CONTENTS

Introduction 4

Characters 6

Man of the Moment

Act One 7
Act Two 62

Additional Material
Alan Ayckbourn: Playwright and Man of the Theatre 105
Interview with Alan Ayckbourn on *Man of the Moment* 110
Interview with "Douglas Beechey" 115

INTRODUCTION

Man of the Moment was first performed at the Stephen Joseph Theatre, Scarborough, in May 1988, directed by the author. It is one of a number of playtexts of the 1980s which Ayckbourn has called his "state-of-the-nation" plays. He refers to some of the titles in the interview included in this edition.

In his plays of the Eighties, the dramatist more explicitly than before deals with questions of public morality, of good and evil in contemporary English society. At the time of writing them, his direct concern with public affairs was a change from the earlier plays, which had focused on family life and the often rather unsatisfactory relations between men and women, the unsatisfactoriness being mainly the men's fault, who are portrayed as thick-skinned, clumsy, unimaginative, and unreliable. But even in those earlier plays there had been a hint of a wider significance, for in watching them we cannot help wondering whether something may be wrong about a society in which people "handle each other in boxing gloves half the time" (*Conversations with Ayckbourn*, ed. Ian Watson [London & Boston: Faber, [2]1988], p. 95). The later plays, the plays of the Eighties, are not "political" in the narrow sense of showing public events or public institutions, like party conferences, election campaigns, cabinet meetings, etc. The settings are the familiar ones of middle-class homes, middle-class families, small groups of friends or partners in business; even the themes of private life, the "relationship" themes, are still there. But the "boxing-gloves" are used with growing skill and bitterness, and sometimes they are replaced by deadlier weapons, like guns – or a tin of baked beans. In the earlier plays, people had problems of communication because they were so self-centred; in his plays of the Eighties, Ayckbourn's characters are downright ruthless and selfish, their lack of sensitivity having changed to aggressiveness, which seems to reflect the new spirit of competitiveness and greed seen as characteristic of English society under the influence of Thatcherism. But in spite of all the underlying seriousness, these plays are still comedies, or at least they manage to keep a remarkable balance between the comic elements and the not so funny ones. Whatever his uneasiness about the "state of the nation", Alan Ayckbourn cannot help noticing, and making us notice, the grotesque and ridiculous side of situations and events that with other writers might develop into full-blown tragedies.

Man of the Moment is a play about human beings under the influence of one of the most powerful public media: television. We cannot be sure all the time about what we see on the stage, or are supposed to see, as audience in a theatre. Are we witnesses of "spontaneous" events happening to the characters on stage just while we are watching them, or have the events we are watching just been arranged by some characters in the play (Jill Rillington and her camera-team) for the purpose of being filmed and watched by other people later on?

But the play is not about the definitions of reality provoked by the tricks of modern electronic media, it is about the moral confusion in our perception of good and evil which results from the specific view of life presented on television. In *Man of the Moment* the former bank-robber, Vic Parks, has become a "star", a great TV personality with several successful shows; the former bank-clerk, Douglas Beechey, who heroically attacked the armed robber and thus helped the police to arrest him, after a very brief period of popularity has been forgotten by the media and by the public; and the beautiful young woman taken hostage and brutally wounded by the robber has ended up as the forgotten ex-bank-clerk's wife, a nervous wreck maimed for life.

This is the situation at the beginning of the play, when an ambitious young TV journalist, Jill Rillington, tries to set up a confrontation between the two former opponents, for a TV series of her own.

Here is the play!

Characters

Vic Parks
Trudy, *his wife*
Cindy, aged seven, *their daughter*
Sharon Giffin, *their children's nanny*
Ruy, *their Spanish gardener*
Marta, Ruy's wife, *their Spanish maid*
Kenny Collins, *Vic's manager*
Jill Rillington
Douglas Beechey
Ashley Barnes, *a TV floor manager*
plus
seven actors (six non-speaking)

Setting: The patio/pool area of Vic's and Trudy's Mediterranean villa.
Time: One day, recently.

nanny a woman looking after little children in a family **floor manager** "stage manager" in a TV studio, director's assistant in charge of all activities on the studio floor and of the studio-audience **patio** terrace, paved outdoor area next to a house

Act One

The paved patio/pool area of a modern, moderate-sized (three-bedroomed) villa in a Spanish-speaking area of the Mediterranean. At one side, a glimpse of the villa itself. White stucco walls and wooden shutters. The edge of the living area – tiled floor with rugs – perhaps the end of what promises to be a very long drinks bar. Large, open sliding doors leading out from the living area on to a shaded area. Here, a table and chairs to seat about four. Moving away from the house further, a step down to a slightly sunken sunbathing area. Here, two or three sun loungers and a low table. At the other side, steps up again to the back gate of the villa, which in turn leads to a carport and the rough road.

Also visible, the raised, angled corner of the swimming pool (deep end). It is possible to walk around the pool, either along the deep end to reach the diving board (unseen) or along the poolside to reach the shallow end. One or two shrubs in tubs. Perhaps a toy left lying about, betraying the presence of young children.

At the start, though, none of this is visible. Just a light on JILL RILLINGTON *who sits on the patio in a chair beside the table angled out facing away from the house.* JILL *is in her early thirties and looking good – certainly at first glance. Every inch the assured, charming TV reporter/presenter.*

stucco white plaster covering walls or ceiling, often decorated with patterns **shutter** extra board or metal covers protecting windows from the outside when they are shut **tiled** covered with tiles (flat bricks of baked clay) **rug** small carpet **to seat** to provide seats for **lounger** *here:* comfortable chair **diving board** a long board by the side of a swimming-pool, from which swimmers can jump into the water **shrub** a bush (like a rose, rhododendron) **tub** a round container **angled out** placed at an angle **presenter** (*TV*) person who is seen on the TV screen presenting the programme to the audience

She is at present doing a piece to camera, though we won't guess this immediately. The film crew are out of sight and remain so throughout. Sometimes we will hear their distant voices calling to JILL *but their words are impossible to decipher.*

JILL (*to camera*) Hallo. I'm Jill Rillington. In this edition of *Their Paths Crossed,* we tell a story that started seventeen years ago in the slow and sneet of a Surrey Novem ... Oh, piss! Keep rolling. We'll go again. Snow and sleet. Snow and sleet ... (*slowly*) Snow – and – sleet ... Here we go. Snow and sleet. Hallo. I'm Rill Jillington ... My God, I don't believe this – Right, straight in – keep turning. Hallo. I'm Jill Rillington. In this edition of *Their Paths Crossed,* we tell a story that started seventeen years ago in the snow and sleet of a Surrey November morning and finishes – (*She gestures. As she does so, the lights spread out to include the whole area, rather as if the camera had pulled back to include her surroundings. We see she is wearing a discreet radio mic attached to her blouse. On the table beside her is a cardboard folder containing research material, press clippings and interview notes.*) – here. In the brilliant sunshine of a glorious Mediterranean summer. It's a story which has – fittingly perhaps – almost a fairy-tale ring to it. A tale with a hero and a villain – even a damsel in distress. But this is no child's fable, it is a true story. This is the real world where nothing is as it seems. This is the real world where heroes are easily forgotten; this is the real world where the villains may, themselves, become heroes. And as for distressed damsels – well, are they in reality ever truly rescued? I'll leave you, the viewer, to judge for yourself ... (*She pauses for a moment, looking towards the camera.*) And – cut! OK?

A shout of assent from the crew.

to camera (*TV*) looking into the camera **to decipher s.th** to work out the meaning of, understand s.th **to roll** (of a camera) to be switched on and working **sleet** rain mixed with bits of ice and snow **to pull back (of a camera)** to change position or focus for a more distant view **discreet** tactful, *here:* not too obviously placed **radio mic** (*techn*) microphone working without wires **folder** cardboard folded to hold writing-paper **research** finding background information on people etc. **press clippings** articles cut from newspapers, press cuttings **ring** *here:* sound, quality **damsel in distress** frightened young woman (in poetry of the Middle Ages) **assent** accepting, saying yes

Did you get the wide? (*gesturing*) The wide?

Crew replies.

Good. Did you get this whole area? (*gesturing and yelling*) This whole area?

A yell from one of the crew.

What? (*She notices her radio mic.*) Oh, yes. Sorry, Dan. Didn't mean to burst your eardrums. Sorry, my love. (*She consults her watch. She makes to yell again then thinks better of it.*) George – (*quietly*) Sorry, love. Dan, can you tell George to set up the arrival shot. For the arrival. Can he do that? Where we talked about? On the bend? So we see this man's taxi coming up the hill and their first meeting at the front door? OK? George knows where. I'll be with you in a sec. Thank you, love. I'll unplug. Save your batteries.

She unplugs her mic from its transmitter in her pocket and tucks away the lead. As she is doing this, TRUDY *comes out from the house rather tentatively. She is only a few years older than Jill but looks rather more. Possibly due to an over-eagerness to please her husband Vic, Trudy has attempted to retain the look of someone ten years younger; an image presumably with which he originally fell in love. She has taken rather more care than usual this morning as the TV cameras are about.*

TRUDY Sorry. Is it all right for me – ?

JILL Yes, we've finished. It's quite all right.

TRUDY Would you all care for coffee? A cup of coffee?

JILL Well, I'de love one. I think the crew are probably OK. They seem to have brought their own – refreshments.

TRUDY Sure?

the wide (*TV*) wide-angle shot **eardrum** membrane inside the ear **to set up** (*TV*) to arrange the equipment for a shot **bend** curve (of a road) **transmitter** (*techn*) (piece of) equipment that sends out radio signals **to tuck s.th. away** to put s.th. safely away, e.g. inside a pocket **lead** wires connecting parts of electrical equipment **tentatively** (*adv*) not sure of oneself, uncertain **presumably** (*adv*) probably, possibly

JILL No, it's probably best to let them get on. We need to set up for this new shot. I want to catch Mr Beechey actually arriving here straight from his hotel …

TRUDY Yes, yes, yes …

JILL And hopefully his first meeting with your husband . . .

TRUDY Yes, yes. I don't know if Vic's . . .

JILL Is he still not back?

TRUDY Well, he should be. He said he would be. (*moving to the gate*) Kenny was going to see if he could … Just a minute, I'll … (*calling to someone*) Kenny, is he coming? Can you see them? No?

JILL No?

TRUDY No, I'm sorry. He only took the children down to the beach. With Sharon. She's their nanny. You can usually see them on the beach down there … He did promise he'd be here …

JILL (*rather coolly*) Yes, he did.

TRUDY It's not like him to do this. I'll make the coffee. It may have just slipped his mind. (*smiling*) Once he gets with the kids …

Trudy hurries back into the house.

JILL (*smiling*) Yes. (*Sourly, looking at her watch again.*) Bugger him.

She is gathering up her folder from the table as KENNY *comes through the back gate. Late twenties or early thirties. He is one of the new breed of young manager/agents with a cool, laid-back, slightly public school, unflappable exterior which just serves to conceal any insecurity beneath.*

KENNY No. No sign.

JILL Well, where is he?

KENNY Digging on the beach. Burying the kids. Bonking the nanny. I don't know.

JILL But he knew about this. He knew …

KENNY Oh, yes, he knew all right.

JILL I mean you knew it, Kenny, we talked about it last night …

KENNY I know, he definitely knew …

bugger him (*taboo sl*) damn him **to gather s.th. up** to pick up **laid-back** sure of oneself, relaxed **unflappable** (*infml*) not nervous under any circumstances **to conceal** to hide **insecurity** lack of confidence **to bonk** (*sl*) to have sex with s.b.

JILL He knew I wanted to catch their first meeting …

KENNY I know, I know …

JILL I needed that on camera. He knew that.

KENNY I know, he knew. He said you'd said it to him, I know …

JILL I said it to him. You know I did.

KENNY I know. He knew, all right, he knew …

JILL Then why the hell isn't he here if he knew?

KENNY I don't know. (*Pause.*) You know Vic.

JILL Yes.

KENNY You can't tell him.

JILL I don't see what makes him so special.

KENNY He's a star, darling. A star. Isn't he? (*Pause.*) He won't let you down. Don't worry.

JILL There's no point in saying that. He just has.

KENNY You can film it later. The meeting. You can mock it up later.

JILL I doubt it.

KENNY Why not? Vic can do that. He's a pro. He's used to that. He did a programme once. Visiting sick kids in hospital. He was 140 miles away in a London studio. No one ever knew. Except the kids he was meant to be visiting. He can do that sort of thing. Piece of cake.

JILL I'm sure Vic could. I'm not so sure about Mr Beechey.

KENNY No?

JILL No.

KENNY Not your television natural, I take it?

JILL He's about as lively as a sheet of laminated chipboard. I've just spent four days interviewing Mr Beechey. In his home town of Purley. I think I've got about twenty seconds of usable material. And those are the shots of Purley.

KENNY Not a talker?

JILL Oh, he talks. It's just he never says anything. You know, when I first started out with the BBC as a radio interviewer, I went on this course and they warned us that one day we'd all of us find ourselves interviewing the uninterviewable. I thought, after ten years, I'd managed to escape. And then along comes

to mock s.th. up to construct a life-size model of **pro** (*infml*) professional **piece of cake** (*infml*) easy to do, like eating a piece of cake **natural** (*n., infml*) person with a natural talent for something **laminated chipboard** (*techn*) board made by combining very small pieces of wood and glue under pressure

Mr Beechey. (*musing*) It's not that he won't talk. You can usually cope with that. We all get that. Then you can generally coax them round. Eventually. Or you say something so blatantly incorrect about them, they're forced to contradict you in self-defence. But this man, he's deadly. The point is, there's absolutely nothing you can say to him that he doesn't agree with. He smothers you with approval. It's like interviewing a fire blanket.

KENNY You normally only meet people like that during general elections, don't you? What about Mrs Beechey? Any joy with her?

JILL She spent the four days we were there hiding in the boxroom. I never got to speak to her at all. All I'm hoping is, once he's here – far away from the bright lights of Purley – he might open up.

KENNY (*wandering to the gate to look*) A little sunshine. Does wonders.

JILL Is Vic coming?

KENNY Can't see him.

JILL Listen, Kenny, I hope he's taking this seriously ...

KENNY Of course. You know Vic. He's a pro ...

JILL I mean, this may just be another tacky little interview as far as he's concerned ...

KENNY He's never said that –

JILL ... a jokey programme which only merits an eighth of his attention ...

KENNY Whoever said that – ?

JILL . . . but for me this is important. It may not seem much to you, but if this works out – then I have their firm provisional promise of the other seven slots. That is eight in all ...

KENNY (*duly impressed*) Eight, heavens!

JILL Plus – plus – wait for it! Plus another pencilled second series of eight in the New Year.

KENNY Sixteen, goodness ...

to muse to think about s.th. **to cope with s.b./s.th.** to deal with s.b./s.th. **to coax s.b. around** to talk to s.b. in a friendly way until he/she gives in **eventually** (*adv*) finally, in the end **blatantly** (*adv*) obviously, crudely **to smother s.b.** to make it impossible for s.b. to breathe, *G.* ersticken **approval** *here:* expression(s) of agreement **fire blanket** (*techn*) special fire-proof blanket used to put out small fires **boxroom** a small room for suitcases etc. **tacky** (*infml, AmE*) insignificant, of poor quality **jokey** (*infml*) humorous **to merit s.th.** to be worth, to deserve **provisional** not final, for the present time only **slot** (*TV*) a position on the schedule of a TV company reserved for a particular programme **duly** (*adv*) properly (as the case deserves) **pencilled** for the time being, provisional

JILL Right. Sixteen. Of my own series. Seventy per cent film – thirty per cent studio – me – nobody else – me alone –

KENNY (*humouring her along*) That's some doing. These days.

JILL Oh, I know a lot of people are sitting back there waiting for me to fall flat on my arse. Colin and Martin thing. Clare. She certainly is. And that Richard – whatsit. They are all dying for that to happen . . . Well, I've got this far and no one is going to trip me up now. I've fought for this chance – just watch me go . . .

KENNY I will. I will ...

JILL Not Mr Beechey, not you, not Vic, not that damp, septic tank of a film crew I've been landed with – and I know who saddled me with them, thank you very much, Mrs McIver, I'll settle you when I get back home, madam, if I don't – God, is this mic still on? No . . . Oh, relief . . . Kenny, if the choice is this or making ten-minute promo videos of eager fringe companies from Stockport for the British Council, I know which I want to do. Just remember Vic owes me, Kenny. He owes me one. I helped him. Remember that. (*pointing to herself*) This kid from BBC Radio Bristol got that whole splendid career of his started. Remember that.

KENNY All right, all right.

JILL Just remember.

KENNY All right. Easy.

Pause. Jill simmers.

We love you. Promise. We're all mad about you.

JILL (*muttering*) I don't want love, I just want basic cooperation, all right?

KENNY (*moving back to the gate*) Relax.

JILL (*looking at her watch again*) He should be here. Why isn't he here? Neither of them are here. This is all I need.

to humour s.b. to keep or make s.b. happy by agreeing to the person's wishes **thing, whatsit** (*infml*) words used for a name or word one cannot remember **dying for** *here:* waiting for **to trip s.b. up** to cause s.b. to fall or stumble **damp** *here:* unenthusiastic, weak **septic tank** (*derog.*) American, "rhyming slang" for Yank(ee) **to saddle s.b. with s.b./s.th.** to get s.b. to do an unpleasant job, or to look after s.b. **to settle s.b.** (*infml*) to deal with s.b., to pay s.b. back, *G.* mit jdm. abrechnen **relief** feeling of relaxation when a pain or worry is over **promo** (*infml*) promotion, advertising **fringe** (*theatre*) unconventional, new **the British Council** organization financed by the British government to support British cultural activities abroad **to owe s.b. (one)** (*infml*) to be obliged to do s.b. a favour in return for an earlier favour or good deed **to simmer** to be almost boiling

KENNY It's only one minute past.

JILL By the time they get here, that film crew will want a break. I've never met anything like them. Every time they change film they have a union meeting. And it's no use trying to do anything after lunch, because they're all totally legless. There's that much camera shake, you'd think we were filming on the top of Mount Etna …

KENNY (*still at the gate*) There's a car in the distance just starting up the hill.

JILL Is it Vic?

KENNY No, it's not the jeep. It looks like a taxi from here. Probably your Mr Beechey.

JILL Right. Well, we can film him arriving, anyway. Get his reactions. If he has any. Keep a look out for Vic. (*as she goes*) You're his agent, get him here.

KENNY His manager …

Jill hurries out through the garden gate.

JILL (*calling*) George! Come on, get a move on. He's coming! Come on, come on!

As Jill goes, Trudy comes out from the house with a tray of coffee things.

TRUDY Is something happening?

KENNY I think Mr Beechey's arrived.

TRUDY (*without enthusiasm*) Oh. Good.

KENNY What's the matter? Nervous?

TRUDY Not at all.

KENNY It was years ago. You weren't even around.

TRUDY You know perfectly well how I feel about all this.

KENNY All right.

TRUDY I blame you. You talked him into it. This programme.

KENNY When have I ever talked Vic into anything? When has anyone? Come on. Don't blame me. Be honest. Have *you*? Have you ever talked him into anything?

Trudy doesn't reply.

(*his point proved*) Well, then.

union (short for) trade union **legless** (*infml*) so drunk that one cannot use one's legs **camera shake** shaking movement of the camera

TRUDY He said he'd be back by now. He's forgotten. I bet that's what's happened. He always forgets what he doesn't choose to remember.

KENNY Sharon might have reminded him.

TRUDY (*with ill-concealed dislike*) Well, I think telling the time's a bit beyond Sharon. I'd better fetch another cup.

(*She makes to leave.*)

KENNY Haven't you got anyone to help you today?

TRUDY How do you mean?

KENNY You know. To make the coffee? Fetch things out?

TRUDY Oh, yes. Marta's here. Only by the time I've explained it to her, it's quicker to do it myself. I mean, she can speak quite good English. I know she can. She always understands Vic. It's just me. She doesn't seem to understand me at all. It's probably the way I talk, I don't know …

Trudy goes back into the house. Kenny wanders to the pool. He stoops and tests the water temperature with his hand. As he is doing this, RUY, *a man in his fifties, comes through the back gate with a pool rake. He ignores Kenny, as he ignores everyone, except on those rare occasions when Vic speaks to him.*

KENNY Good morning to you.

Ruy totally ignores him. He starts to rake the surface of the pool. This activity soon takes him out of view.

(*sarcastically, in response to Ruy's lack of response*) Thank you. And the same to you. Lovely chatting to you. Now, you must excuse me interrupting but I have to get on. Not at all. And the same to you.

Trudy enters from the house.

TRUDY (*talking to someone following behind her*) We're just about to have coffee out here. If you'd care to join us …

ill-concealed badly hidden **beyond** too dificult for **pool rake** a tool with a long handle to clean the surface of the water of leaves etc. **in response** answering, reacting to

Trudy is followed by DOUGLAS BEECHEY, *a man in his early forties. He is, as Jill has hinted, quite staggeringly unimpressive on first acquaintance. He is, though, as with many of nature's creatures, compensated for his apparent total lack of aggression by an almost complete invulnerability to attack by others. His clothes are quite unsuited to the climate.*

DOUGLAS (*as he approaches*) Isn't this glorious? Isn't this simply glorious . . . (*stopping in the doorway to survey the patio and pool*) Oh, now. This is glorious.

TRUDY (*unsure how to react*) Thank you. May I introduce (*indicating Kenny*) – have you met my husband's manager?

KENNY (*stepping towards them*) How do you do?

TRUDY This is Kenneth Collins. Mr Beechey.

DOUGLAS Douglas Beechey. How do you do?

KENNY Kenny Collins. Good to meet you.

They shake hands.

DOUGLAS Isn't this glorious? Isn't this just glorious? May I – (*He indicates the terrace.*)

TRUDY (*waving him in*) Of course.

DOUGLAS (*exploring the area*) Oh. Oh. Oh. Oh. (*admiring the view from the garden gate*) Oh. (*investigating the pool*) Oh. Look at this pool. Doesn't that look inviting?

TRUDY You're welcome to have a swim, any time.

DOUGLAS No, I don't swim.

TRUDY No?

DOUGLAS No, no. Me and water, I'm afraid, we've never seen eye to eye. (*calling to the unseen Ruy*) Hallo. Good morning to you.

TRUDY I was just fetching another cup. Excuse me.

DOUGLAS Of course. May I help at all . . . ?

TRUDY No, no. Wait there.

Trudy goes back into the house.

DOUGLAS Well, I must say. Who could ask for anything more, eh?

KENNY Yes.

DOUGLAS Glorious. Quite glorious. (*indicating in Ruy's direction*) Who's that? Is he one of the family?

staggeringly (*adv*) extremely **invulnerability** impossibility of being wounded **to investigate s.th** to examine **to see eye to eye** to agree

KENNY No, that's the gardener.

DOUGLAS (*impressed*) Oh. The gardener. I see.

KENNY Right.

DOUGLAS Very impressive. (*looking around*) All you need now is a garden, eh? (*He laughs.*)

KENNY Well, I think he cleans the pool and – odd jobs, you know –

DOUGLAS Oh, yes, I'm sure. I was only joking. I expect this paving would need weeding to start with. I should imagine. I suppose they get weeds here, don't they? Same as we do?

KENNY I would imagine so.

DOUGLAS (*calling to Ruy*) Excuse me, I say . . . Do you get weeds? I say! Do you have weeds here?

KENNY I don't think he speaks much English.

DOUGLAS Oh. (*calling*) *Gracias!* (*to Kenny*) That's the only bit of Spanish I know.

KENNY Pretty impressive.

DOUGLAS I definitely don't know the Spanish for weed killer, that's for certain. (*breathing in the air*) Glorious! (*Slight pause.*)

KENNY Good flight?

DOUGLAS Pardon?

KENNY Good flight? Out here? On the aeroplane? Did you have a good one?

DOUGLAS Oh, glorious. I was with a very jolly crowd from Dagenham. Singing their heads off, all the way over.

KENNY Oh, yes?

DOUGLAS When they weren't playing practical jokes on the crew, that was. You had to laugh.

KENNY Sounds fun.

DOUGLAS Couple of them dressed up as air hostesses. Couple of the men. Then it turned out we were all staying in the same hotel. So …

KENNY That OK? The hotel?

DOUGLAS Very clean. And the windows open. That's all I ever ask for in a hotel.

KENNY (*slightly baffled*) Really?

odd jobs small jobs, mixture of different jobs **paving** paved area, area covered with carefully fitted flat stones **to weed** to clear the garden of weeds (unwanted plants) **weed killer** powder or liquid used by gardeners to remove weeds **practical joke** non-verbal joke, amusing trick played on s.b. **baffled** confused, not understanding

DOUGLAS I need air to sleep, you see. Not that I stay in them very often. Oh, I'm savouring every minute of this, I can tell you. Free trip. Free meals. Free hotel. VIP treatment. And appearing on the television. You don't get that every day, do you?

KENNY You certainly don't.

DOUGLAS Make the most of it, I say.

KENNY I should.

DOUGLAS I see they were all out there to greet my arrival. The film crew. I got to know them all quite well. While they were sitting in our front room for four days. Good to see them again. All out there. Filming away. And dear old Jill, waving her arms about as usual. She doesn't half go at them sometimes. Mind you, they take it all in very good part. They're a very pleasant bunch. Very easy-going, I've found. Well, let's put it this way, we certainly had a few good laughs while they were in Purley. (*He has moved back to stand by the garden gate.*) That'll be the Mediterranean Sea? Down there? Right?

KENNY The bit covered in water. Where the land stops.

DOUGLAS (*surveying the view thoughtfully*) The Med, eh? Well, well. That's something else I can tell people I've seen.

Trudy returns with the extra cup.

TRUDY Here we are.

DOUGLAS Well, I can't say I'm not a tinge green, Mrs Parks. I must say, this is just perfection.

TRUDY Yes, we're very – lucky.

KENNY (*anxious to correct any wrong impression*) Mind you, you didn't get it for nothing, did you? You've earned it.

DOUGLAS (*anxious to do the same*) Oh, yes.

TRUDY Well, Vic earned it.

KENNY You both have.

TRUDY (*smiling, unconvinced*) It's nice of you to say so.

DOUGLAS Behind every successful man, don't they say?

TRUDY I'm afraid my husband's still on the beach with the children. He should be back shortly.

DOUGLAS Oh, how many children have you?

TRUDY Two. Coffee, Mr Beechey?

to savour s.th. to enjoy the taste of s.th. **front room** living-room **not half** (*infml*) not at all **to take s.th. in good part** to accept s.th. in a good mood **bunch** (*infml*) group **easy-going** not worrying **tinge** slight degree, nuance **green/green with envy** (*infml*) jealous

DOUGLAS Thank you. Do call me Douglas, won't you? Milk and three sugars, thank you.

TRUDY Kenny?

KENNY Please. Usual. Black, no sugar.

DOUGLAS And how old are the children, Trudy – may I call you Trudy?

TRUDY Cindy is seven and Timmy is just five.

DOUGLAS Lovely. One of each, then?

TRUDY Yes.

DOUGLAS They must love it out here.

TRUDY Oh, yes, they do. (*offering him coffee*) Mr Beechey.

DOUGLAS Thank you. Douglas. Please. Call me Douglas.

Slight pause, Kenny is served coffee.

KENNY Thanks. Do you have children, Mr – Douglas?

DOUGLAS No. No. (*A slight pause as if he might be going to say something else.*) No.

KENNY Ah.

DOUGLAS My wife was – Well, we made a joint decision not to have any. We decided we weren't ideal parent material. Either of us.

KENNY It's a pity your wife couldn't come with you.

DOUGLAS Oh, no. Nerys is not a traveller.

KENNY No?

DOUGLAS I'm afraid this sort of trip would be quite beyond her.

KENNY Oh. What a shame.

Pause.

TRUDY She's – She's all right, is she? I mean, she's not ill, your wife?

DOUGLAS Oh, no. She's very chirpy.

KENNY Oh, grand.

DOUGLAS At present. She has her ups and downs, of course.

TRUDY Don't we all?

KENNY Absolutely.

Pause.

joint (*fml*) done in cooperation **chirpy** (*infml*) cheerful **ups and downs** phases of happiness and depression

TRUDY You'll appreciate that I'm Vic's second wife. I wasn't around when – when all that happened – I mean, Vic and I, we've only been married eight years.

DOUGLAS Yes, I did read he'd remarried. I read all about your romance. In his book.

TRUDY (*not pleased*) Did you?

DOUGLAS Sounded very romantic. Is that how it actually was? Did he really abduct you from the middle of a public car park in the back of a transit van?

TRUDY (*reluctantly*) Well, sort of, yes ...

KENNY Mind you, Trudy was standing around for some time waiting to be abducted. weren't you?

Douglas laughs. Another pause.

TRUDY No, what I'm saying is that – all that happened – all that – between you – happened while Vic was married to Donna, you see. I was not around then. I didn't even know him. I was married to somebody else as well, as it happens. Only that didn't work out.

DOUGLAS That would be your previous marriage to the dental mechanic?

TRUDY Yes ...

DOUGLAS Oh, dear ...

TRUDY (*faintly irritated*) No, what I'm saying is, I had nothing to do with that part of Vic's life. If they want to know about that – for this programme – then they'll have to ask Donna. Providing they can sober her up. By the time I met Vic that was all in the past. I wasn't a part of it and I don't really want to know about it. We're all different people now. At least I hope we are. And I have to say that I don't agree with this programme anyway. I don't honestly think they should be doing it. I'm sorry. I've said it to Vic and I've said it to her. That Jill Rillington. And now I'm saying it to you. I'm sorry. I think it's unnecessary. And hurtful. I think it's raking over old ground and opening old wounds. I'm not at all surprised your wife isn't here. If I were her, I certainly wouldn't be here. Not after what she – Still. As I say, I'm an outsider. I wasn't even around when it happened. And what Vic

to appreciate s.th. *here:* to realize, understand s.th. **to abduct s.b.** to kidnap s.b. **transit van** type of middle-sized delivery van **reluctantly** with hesitation **dental mechanic** person making false teeth **hurtful** painful **to rake over** to bring up forgotten things

does is his own affair. But I am his wife and I think I might have been consulted. I'm also the mother of his children – though you wouldn't think so sometimes, would you? (*She is suddenly on the verge of crying.*) Excuse me. I just have to fetch some – things …

Trudy hurries into the house. Douglas rises, amazed. Kenny remains seated.

Kenny (*calling calmly after her*) Trudy … love … (*Silence.*) She'll be all right.

Douglas Oh, dear. I had no idea she felt … I mean, I wouldn't …

Kenny She'll be fine. Don't worry. Things are just a bit (*he gestures*) – you know …

Douglas How do you mean?

Kenny Between them. Her and Vic.

Douglas Oh …

Kenny Just at the moment. Temporarily. Nothing at all, really. Vic's a bit of a lad sometimes. I mean, I've known them both for ages. They're terrific people. Both of them. I should know. It was me who introduced them.

many lies

Douglas Did you really? That wasn't in the book.

Kenny Vic was just – getting going, you know, after – after his leave of absence – and he took me on – initially as his agent – and later on, as he got in greater demand, I became his personal manager. I got him his first weekly TV slot – regional, mind you – sort of local *Crimewatch/Police Five* sort of thing, you know – scare the old ladies off to bed type of show – and Trudy was a friend of the producer's secretary or somesuch. And. Romance, romance.

Douglas I hope this programme hasn't created a tension between them.

Kenny No, no, no … Why on earth should it? Nice plug for Vic. Nice holiday for you – as you say – all expenses paid. Who's it hurting? I mean, your wife didn't object, did she? And she has far

on the verge of nearly **temporarily** (*adv*) for a limited time only **terrific** (*infml*) wonderful, great **leave of absence** (*fml*) permission to be absent from work or duty, holiday **initially** at the beginning **in demand** wanted, wished for **Crimewatch** a TV programme like *XY ungelöst* **scare the old ladies off to bed type of show** the type of show that will frighten old ladies so much that they will run away and hide in their beds **tension** nervousness **plug** (*infml*) act of promotion, of creating publicity

more reason to than Trudy, hasn't she? But your wife's presumably perfectly happy for you to be here?

DOUGLAS Well, Nerys had initial objections, I have to say. And she certainly didn't want to be any part of it herself. Although Jill Rillington did try very hard to persuade her to be interviewed. But Nerys said if I wanted to do it and Vic Parks wanted to do it, then who was she … I mean, the way Jill described the programme to me, I think it's a very interesting idea, don't you? What's happened to us all since. Since …

KENNY Oh, you bet …

DOUGLAS Take Vic, for instance. He has had the most amazing career, hasn't he? Considering.

KENNY Oh, incredible …

DOUGLAS I mean, from what he was then – to what he is now. He's an example to us all, isn't he? …

KENNY He is.

DOUGLAS A remarkable man. You have to admire him. What he's done. Particularly for the young people. And all that from nothing.

KENNY Less than that really.

DOUGLAS Absolutely.

Slight pause.

KENNY I suppose quite a lot must have happened to you, as well? In, what is it, seventeen years? You must have seen some changes in your own life.

DOUGLAS One or two. (*He reflects.*) Not many really. I married Nerys, of course. And I changed my job. Well, I could hardly have continued at the bank.

KENNY Memories too painful, were they?

DOUGLAS No, no. But people used to come in just to stare at me, you know. While we were trying to conduct bank business. And Mr Marsh – that was my manager at the time – he's retired now to Bournemouth – he felt my presence was not conducive to normal, satisfactory banking practices and he offered to request a transfer for me to another district. But I couldn't in all conscience leave Purley – I was born and bred there, you see – so I left the bank altogether. And then, hey presto, I was lucky

conducive (to) causing, encouraging s.th. **to request s.th.** (*frml*) to ask for s.th.
hey presto a magician's formula used before a trick

enough to land a job straightaway with a local firm of double-glazing consultants, and I've been book-keeping for them ever since. Not an earth-shattering tale, perhaps, but one with a happy ending none the less.

KENNY And a success story, too. In its own way.

DOUGLAS True. True. Nerys and I are both happy, anyway. That's the main thing.

KENNY And you've both got your health and strength.

DOUGLAS And we've both got our health and strength, precisely. Well, Nerys is sometimes ... But it's mostly in her mind. I've told her she looks fine. She really does. Her face is fine.

KENNY Why, she's not – is she – still disfigured, is she?

DOUGLAS Oh, no, no, no. All there is – if you look very carefully, she's got the faintest traces of scar tissue, just around here (*he indicates the side of his face*) – but you really couldn't tell, I promise. He did a marvellous job, that surgeon. One of the best of his day, he was – he's dead now, alas. Died last year –

KENNY Oh, sad ...

DOUGLAS But if she wears the make-up, it's undetectable. No one could tell.

KENNY Fine, then ...

DOUGLAS The trouble is, Nerys won't always trouble with the make-up. She can't always be bothered. So then she goes out to the shops and people start staring at her – or she imagines they're staring at her anyway – I don't honestly think, myself, they bother to give her a second look, if you want the truth, still ... Then she comes home upset and she won't go out of the house for months on end. I've said to her, Nerys, if you'd only wear the make-up, you wouldn't have all this upset, would you?

KENNY A lot of women wear make-up.

DOUGLAS They do. I've told her that.

KENNY Most women wear make-up.

DOUGLAS Yes. I mean, this is a special make-up, it has to be said. It's slightly thicker than normal. But it's the same principle. It's like I imagine they must wear on the television. Like dancers must wear. I expect.

KENNY Right.

to land a job to be lucky in finding a good job **double-glazing** windows made up of two sheets of glass **consultant** *here:* an expert salesman **disfigured** having a spoilt appearance, *G.* entstellt **scar tissue** skin growing over a wound **undetectable** not to be seen, hidden

DOUGLAS I mean, if she was a man, I'd have understood her reluctance …

KENNY Oh, yes. If you were a man you wouldn't necessarily want to go strolling about in make-up, would you?

DOUGLAS Not in Purley you wouldn't, certainly. But a woman.

Jill comes on through the garden gate. She is evidently angry.

JILL Sod them. They are useless. They are worse than useless.

DOUGLAS (*rising*) Hallo, Jill …

JILL (*grimly*) Hallo, Mr Beechey. We may have to ask you to arrive all over again. We were just a little slow catching you first time around …

DOUGLAS Right-oh, Jill. Just say the word. (*to Kenny*) I'm getting rather expert at this filming. She had me walking in and out of our kitchen, must have been thirty-five times one day. (*laughingly to Jill*) It was about that, wasn't it?

JILL (*unamused*) At least thirty-five. Is this coffee?

KENNY Help yourself. Trudy's just – just … doing something or other.

Jill helps herself to coffee.

DOUGLAS I did a very good sprint round the local park for you, though, didn't I? We got that in one take, didn't we? I'm looking forward to seeing that. I ran for miles, Kenneth, you've no idea. Nearly killed me. Go on, the crew kept shouting, keep going. (*He laughs.*) I'm looking forward to that.

JILL Well, we may have to leave that bit out, Mr Beechey –

DOUGLAS Oh, dear.

JILL We've got so much wonderful stuff already.

DOUGLAS The crew will be disappointed. It was their idea, wasn't it?

JILL Yes. (*beaming at him with her best professional smile*) Anyway. You're here. That's the main thing. What are your first impressions then, Mr Beechey? Of this place?

KENNY Glorious.

JILL (*irritably*) What?

sod them (*infml, exclamation of anger*) curse them **to beam (at s.b.)** to put on one's most charming smile

DOUGLAS Quite right. Glorious. I couldn't have put it better myself. I must say, I've always heard tell of the dazzling world of show business, but this is the first time I've ever experienced it.

JILL You wouldn't mind it yourself?

DOUGLAS I certainly wouldn't.

JILL How do you feel about someone like, say, Vic having it?

DOUGLAS Lucky him, that's what I say.

JILL You don't feel it's wrong that he should have something like this and you don't?

DOUGLAS I'm sorry, I don't quite follow, how do you mean? Is that a socialist question ...?

KENNY What are you trying to get him to say, Jilly?

DOUGLAS Because I'm not a socialist. Actually, I'm not quite sure what I am just at present. The past few years I have been consciously withholding my vote –

JILL So you don't feel just a little bit jealous?

DOUGLAS Certainly not.

JILL Not the teeniest bit?

DOUGLAS No.

JILL Honestly?

KENNY Jill, the man's just said, he's not jealous –

DOUGLAS (*cheerfully*) Oh, don't worry. She's always going on at me like this ...

JILL I'm sorry, I simply cannot believe that after what happened Mr Beechey can sit here among all this – wealth – these spoils of the good life –

KENNY Come on, Jilly, it's one poky, run-of-the-mill villa in the middle of hundreds – it's no big deal –

JILL Maybe not to you or Vic or me it isn't. But to someone like Mr Beechey, it's beyond his wildest dreams ...

KENNY What are you talking about? This place is littered with people like Mr Beechey –

DOUGLAS Do call me Douglas, please ...

KENNY The place is populated by Mr Beecheys. You can barely move for Beecheys, don't talk nonsense.

dazzling glamorous **teeniest** (*children's language*) tiny, very small **to go on at s.b.** to attack s.b. with words **spoils** (*fml, lit*) the goods one takes away from an enemy in war **poky** (*infml derog*) very small, very narrow **run-of-the-mill** (*adj, infml*) ordinary **littered (with)** untidily covered (with)

JILL (*angrily indicating Douglas*) If you had seen – if you had seen, by contrast, the dingy little house this man is forced to live in. On the edge of a roaring main trunk road – rooms the size of this table – fading wallpaper … worn carpets … God! (*She shudders.*) Sorry, Mr Beechey, but …

DOUGLAS (*without offence*) We're really both quite fond of it, actually.

JILL (*calming down*) Just don't try and kid me he wouldn't prefer this if he were given a choice …

KENNY And all I'm saying is, don't hold this place up as some fantastic dream palace. It's a perfectly ordinary holiday shack. A lot of people have one. Most people have one. If they've bothered to save up …

Slight pause.

DOUGLAS Mind you, I think we've got used to that house over the years. You don't notice the little drawbacks quite so much after a while. I must be honest, we have meant to do something about that hall carpet for some years. But it's getting a good match with the stairs, you see. That's the problem. They don't really make that mauve any more. It means I have to keep bringing the samples home with me – because, of course, Nerys can't face walking into Debenhams, certainly not on a Saturday morning.

A silence.

KENNY The man is just not the jealous type, Jill, forget it.

JILL (*with ill-concealed annoyance*) So you have no feelings at all about this place, Mr Beechey? Like you appear not to have feelings about anything very much?

DOUGLAS Oh, I have feelings, Jill, I most certainly do. Very deep feelings. But I sincerely hope that envy is not one of them. Because envy in my book is a deadly sin and as a practising Christian, that is something I try to avoid.

JILL Super. I'm glad to hear it. Well, perhaps you ought to tell me something you do feel strongly about and we'll try and include that in the programme.

dingy dirty, dark **trunk road** long-distance road **to fade** to lose colour and brightness **offence** the feeling of having been insulted, hurt **to kid s.b.** (*infml*) to fool s.b. **shack** hut; small, simple house **drawback** weak point, disadvantage **mauve** pale mix of blue and red, *G.* malvenfarben **Debenhams** chain of department stores

KENNY Jill, come on …

JILL Illegal parking on double yellow lines? Any good? Dogs fouling footpaths? Free double glazing for senior citizens?

DOUGLAS (*thoughtfully*) I suppose evil, really.

JILL Evil?

DOUGLAS Yes. I feel strongly about that.

JILL That's it? Just evil?

DOUGLAS Yes. Only, it's often hard to recognize. But there's a lot of it about, you know.

A silence. Suddenly, there in the garden gateway stands VIC PARKS. *A powerful man in his late forties. He has just come from the beach and is wearing shorts, sports shirt and canvas beach shoes. Holding shyly on to his hand is his elder child* CINDY, *a pretty little girl of seven. The others don't immediately see him.*

VIC Good morning. Don't we say good morning, then?

Jill and Douglas rise. Kenny follows suit, rather more slowly.

JILL (*delightedly*) Vic …

DOUGLAS (*obediently*) Good morning …

KENNY (*with them*) About time …

VIC (*gently*) Cindy, you get changed and then you take Timmy up the other end of the pool, all right? And look after him, OK?

Cindy runs off again.

(*shouting after her*) And do what Sharon says. You listen to Sharon, all right?

JILL (*embracing him*) Hallo, Vic.

VIC Hallo, how's my girl?

JILL Grateful you've decided to turn up.

VIC Well, where are the cameras, then? Where're the cameras? I thought this place would be a mass of people. Cameras, sound men, extra lighting rigs … Look at it, I ask you. Bugger all. I make my special entrance. Get dressed up specially …

double yellow lines lines along the road forbidding parking **to foul** *here:* to make dirty by leaving excrement **gateway** opening in fence or hedge **canvas** strong cloth of which sails or tents are made **lighting rig** set of lights

JILL I sent them off to do the mute shots. They'll be back in an hour –

VIC They'd better be. I came all the way up from the beach for this – (*to Douglas*) How do you do, Vic Parks. You'll be –

JILL This is Douglas Beechey –

DOUGLAS Hallo. Great to meet you. I'm a real fan –

VIC Well, that's very nice to hear. (*to Jill*) Listen, you'll get the kids in somewhere, won't you? Just one shot, eh?

JILL Oh, sure ...

VIC Only I promised Timmy and Cindy they'd be on the telly, you see ...

JILL I was hoping you would let us use them ...

VIC Just one shot. (*to Douglas*) Have you got kids?

DOUGLAS No, no. But I watch your programme. I watch *Ask Vic* every Tuesday –

VIC (*to Kenny*) Now, isn't that interesting? Here's another example ...

Ruy, who has finished raking the swimming pool, has entered and is crossing to the back gate.

Morning, Ruy, lad –

RUY (*cheerily animated*) Hallo, good morning, Mr Vic!

VIC (*to Jill and Douglas*) You know, they did a survey as to what categories of kids make up the viewing sample for *Ask Vic* and they actually found that – 15 per cent, wasn't it?

KENNY Thirteen and a half –

VIC Nearly 15 per cent of our viewers were adults over the age of twenty-one –

KENNY Age of eighteen –

VIC Isn't that incredible?

DOUGLAS Incredible.

VIC No, you think about it for a minute. That's a big percentage, that is, 15 per cent.

DOUGLAS Amazing.

VIC Whereas my evening show – *The Vic Parks Show* – that is exclusively adult. Well, point-oh-one per cent kids, or some-

mute silent, soundless **telly** (*infml*) television **survey** opinion poll **sample** part or group representing the whole **incredible** unbelievable, amazing **point oh-one per cent** 0.01%

thing. So there's no cross spill the other way. Which I find very interesting.

KENNY It is on at eleven o'clock at night, of course –

VIC No. Even so.

DOUGLAS Yes, it's a bit late for me, that one –

VIC What, early riser, are you? (*Claps him on the back.*) Nothing like it. We were down there at what, six-thirty this morning. Magic. Best time to be on a beach. First thing in the morning. Virgin sand, sun coming up, not too hot, clear blue sea ... Now, have you all got what you want? Drink? Food? Anything? Where's Trudy? Isn't she looking after you? I told her to look after you. (*calling into the house*) Trudy! Where is she?

KENNY Trudy's just –

> SHARON GIFFIN *has entered from the garden gate. A girl of about nineteen. Overweight and sadly graceless. She is at present in a sulk. She carries a couple of baskets with towels, toys, etc., which presumably they've brought back from the beach. She is wearing a wetsuit top under her beach robe.*

VIC Sharon, find Trudy. Tell her to come out here.

SHARON (*flatly*) Yes, Mr Parks.

DOUGLAS (*to Sharon*) Hallo, I'm Douglas.

SHARON (*all but ignoring him*) Hallo.

Sharon goes into the house.

JILL We're being looked after fine, Vic. You don't have to worry about us –

VIC No, I can't stand guests being left on their own. That's terrible. I can't stand that. (*feeling the coffee pot*) This is cold and all. (*yelling*) Marta! Marta! Sitting here drinking cold coffee. What the hell's going on here? Marta! Come out here. Sit down. Go on. Sit down.

cross (*adj*) going across **spill** *here:* section of people acting differently from the rest of their group **virgin** (*adj*) fresh, unused **graceless** unattractive, clumsy, esp. referring to movement **in a sulk** in a bad mood **wetsuit** rubber suit for diving, surfing, etc. **top** upper part **beach robe** kind of coat worn on beach **flatly** (of voice, *adv*) dull, disappointed

They sit. MARTA, *a Spanish woman in her fifties, enters in a hurry from the house. Normally dark and brooding but, as with her husband Ruy, in the presence of Vic she is effusive and charming.*

MARTA Yes, Mr Vic?

VIC Marta, coffee. More coffee. Hot. More cups. Clean. Quickly. All right?

MARTA (*taking the tray from the table*) More coffee, more cups.

VIC Hot coffee. Understand?

MARTA Hot coffee.

VIC Hot not cold.

MARTA (*hurring away*) Hot not cold. Yes, Mr Vic.

Marta goes. Vic sits at last, like someone about to hold court. Douglas is holding his old coffee cup. The occasional child's shout is heard from the direction of the swimming pool.

VIC Now then – that's sorted that out … (*seeing the children*) Look at those two. Look at those kids.

DOUGLAS (*smiling appreciatively*) Ah …

VIC You got kids, have you?

DOUGLAS Er – no …

VIC Have some. You don't know what you're missing. (*indicating Douglas's cup*) Leave that, she's fetching some more –

Douglas puts his cup down again, obediently.

(*indicating Kenny*) I'm always telling him that. Kenny. He should have some.

KENNY (*uneasily*) Well, it's tricky …

JILL Kenny's gay, Vic. He doesn't want kids.

VIC Why not? What obstacle's that? These days? Being a poof?

KENNY Quite a bit actually. Anyway, I hate kids, I loathe the sight of them.

VIC (*to Jill*) You should have some, too.

JILL No, thanks. I'll enjoy other people's kids. Much nicer.

VIC (*only just joking*) It's unnatural not to. Every woman who can should have kids. Like every man who can should grow a beard.

brooding thoughtful, reserved **effusive** too emotional **to hold court** like a king **appreciatively** (*adv*) *here:* acknowledging the good qualities **poof** (*derog.*) homosexual man **to loathe s.b./s.th.** to dislike s.b./s.th. very much

Everything you can do you ought to do. Before you die. That's what we're here for. Right?

JILL Tell you what, I'll grow my armpits and you have the baby, OK?

VIC (*mock disgusted*) Dear, oh, dear. Right. What's the plan? (*to Jill*) You're going to make us two into telly stars, are you?

He winks at Douglas. Douglas laughs appreciatively.

JILL I thought the best way to go about this, Vic – with your approval, of course – is this morning, as soon as the boys come back, I'll pick up one or two mute shots here. But perhaps we could spend now, we three, just briefly talking about what we want to talk about. And then this afternoon – (*She hesitates as Vic rises and moves towards the house.*) This after-

VIC Carry on, Jill. Carry on, I'm listening ...

JILL (*having to shout rather as Vic disappears*) This afternoon, I could start by talking with the two of you, just to contrast how you've both fared over seventeen years –

VIC (*off, calling*) Trudy! Trudy! (*calling back to Jill*) Seventeen years, yes, I'm listening ...

JILL (*battling on*) And perhaps – I don't want to dwell on it too much – perhaps just recalling the last meeting between you both.

VIC (*off*) Where are my bloody cigars?

TRUDY (*off*) They're in the drawer, there.

VIC (*off*) They are not in the drawer.

TRUDY (*off*) Well, they were there.

VIC (*off*) Look at that. Look. Is that in the drawer? Is that what's meant by in the drawer?

TRUDY (*off*) I know where they are, just a minute ...

VIC (*off*) Well, bring them out here. We're trying to talk out here. Come on out. (*Vic re-enters from the house.*) Sorry, Jilly, sorry. I apologize. Carry on. (*Jill opens her mouth to do so.*) No, sorry, excuse me – before you do, let me say – Doug – Duggie – can I call you Doug?

DOUGLAS (*delighted*) Yes, of course –

armpits the hollow space under one's arms, below the shoulders **to wink at s.b.** to close one eye briefly as sign of humour or irony **to fare** to get on, be successful or not **to battle** to struggle, keep up an argument

VIC Doug – this girl – discovered me. Can you believe that? This little kid – ankle socks – how old were you, then? Seventeen, something like that –

JILL (*rather coyly*) - was older than that ...

KENNY Twenty-three, you were twenty-three when you met Vic –

JILL Something like that.

VIC This girl – she was – what? You were a local radio interviewer, weren't you?

JILL Right.

VIC I'd just – like, come out, you know – and she's doing this programme about – what was it? *Old Lags' Hour* or something, wasn't it?

Vic winks at Douglas. Douglas laughs appreciatively. The whole of the following gets related rather for his benefit.

No, seriously, it was a programme called – let me see *Facing Things* – right?

KENNY *Facing Up*, it was called.

JILL *Facing Up*.

VIC *Facing Up*, he's right –

JILL About long-term prisoners coming to terms –

VIC With the outside world ...

JILL And this man, his first time on radio –

VIC The very first time I'd ever been on, this is –

JILL By the time we'd finished I'd got enough tape for about twenty-five programmes ...

VIC And then when I'm leaving – you left out the best bit – just when I'm leaving, wasn't it?

JILL Oh, yes, right – and then just as he's leaving – leaving the studio – I'm absolutely exhausted by now, mind you – and he turns to me and he says –

VIC (*laughing*) I said to her, what about my book then?

JILL He says, you never asked me about my book.

Jill, Vic and Kenny laugh. Douglas joins in, though it's clear he doesn't know what they're all laughing about.

ankle socks very short socks **coy(ly)** (*adv*) pretending to be shy or modest **old lag** (*infml*) hardened criminal, (ex-)prisoner **to relate s.th** to tell s.th. **to face up** to be honest

He's only written a bloody book as well …

VIC *My Life* by Vic Parks. Written during Her Majesty's Pleasure – and on Her Majesty's stationery.

KENNY (*to Douglas*) His biography.

DOUGLAS Oh, yes …

KENNY The first one, that was –

VIC The authorized version. It was a shocker, wasn't it?

KENNY Not the one you've read –

VIC No, that's the second one he must have read.

KENNY That was *Life as a Straight Man.*

VIC That only came out a year ago.

KENNY Eighteen months –

DOUGLAS It seemed to be very popular at the library. There was quite a waiting list at the Purley Branch –

VIC Five months at number one … Can't be bad.

DOUGLAS And you wrote that yourself? I mean, that was actually yourself writing, was it?

VIC Er, more or less. More or less. They were mostly my words. That's fair to say, isn't it?

KENNY That's no lie.

VIC There was just – someone else putting them in the right order for me.

KENNY A little bit of help from John.

VIC A little bit of help from John. Bless him. How is he, by the way?

KENNY Much better.

VIC Good. Good. Give him my love.

Trudy comes out with a box of cigars and some matches.

TRUDY Here you are.

VIC Ta. Sit down, sit down.

TRUDY No, I –

VIC Sit down. We're just remembering my first book. Did you ever read that?

TRUDY (*sitting, rather reluctantly*) No, I never read that one.

VIC (*to Jill*) It was a shocker, wasn't it? I don't know how I had the nerve to show it –

stationery writing paper **straight** honest, responsible, non-criminal **branch** *here:* local division **ta** (*infml*) thank you

JILL Don't knock it, now. That started you off, that book.

VIC No, that was you, my darling. You started me off.

KENNY She recognized star quality ...

VIC It was no thanks to that bloody book. I tried that, you know, with – must have been twenty-five publishers –

JILL But it was you reading that book that started your career. I mean, if some producer hadn't heard you reading it on *Pick of the Week*, you'd never have got on *Start the Week*. And if you hadn't done *Start the Week* they'd never have asked you to do *Stop the Week*, would they?

KENNY Or *Any Questions* ...

VIC (*modestly*) True.

KENNY Or *The Book Programme*. Or *Did you See ... ?*

VIC True, true ...

KENNY And the rest is history ...

JILL Absolutely true.

Pause, whilst they all consider Vic's mercurial rise to fame. Marta comes out with a tray of fresh coffee and five cups. Trudy pours coffee during the next. Marta hovers behind her. The sound of the children's shouts from the far end of the pool.

VIC (*shouting to them*) Be careful now. Be careful, Cindy. Now, don't push him.

TRUDY Are they all right?

VIC They're all right.

TRUDY Where's Sharon? Shouldn't she be with them?

VIC She's getting changed, I think.

TRUDY She should be with them ...

VIC They're all right. Don't fuss. I'm keeping an eye on them. (*to Douglas*) You got kids, did you say?

DOUGLAS No ...

VIC You like them, though?

DOUGLAS Oh, yes ...

VIC Look at them. Look at those two ... I love kids. Do you know what I'd do to people who hurt kids?

DOUGLAS No.

to knock s.b./s.th. to criticize s.b./s.th. **pick** (of) choice, best (of) **mercurial** quick **to hover** to be waiting **to fuss** to be nervous, to worry too much

VIC I'd sit them, naked, astride barbed wire ...

DOUGLAS (*wincing slightly*) Ah ...

TRUDY (*irritated by Marta's presence behind her*) Thank you, Marta, I can manage, thank you.

VIC No, let her serve round. She's waiting to serve round, Trudy ...

TRUDY I can serve round.

VIC No, let her. That's her job. That's what she's paid for. We're paying her to serve round. (*to Marta*) Go on. Serve round, you silly cow. Serve them round.

MARTA (*a flashing smile*) Yes, Mr Vic.

VIC We're paying her. We might as well use the bloody woman. Like buying a light bulb and sitting in the dark otherwise, isn't it?

Vic winks at Douglas. Douglas laughs rather more weakly. Trudy has poured out all the coffee and, during the next, Marta circulates with the tray, allowing the guests to serve themselves with cream and sugar.

Anyway. (*to Jill*) You still haven't told us, sweetheart, have you, what your grand plan of campaign is. We await your plan.

JILL Well, I was trying to –

VIC (*about to light a cigar*) Cigar, anyone? Cigar?

They decline.

Sorry, excuse me, carry on.

JILL I thought that the three of us could do an initial three-handed interview this afternoon. Out here, if that's OK –

VIC What? You, me and him, you mean?

JILL Right.

VIC Right. Carry on.

JILL I'd like to use that to discuss, principally, how both your lives have changed over seventeen years –

VIC How long have you got? (*He laughs.*)

JILL Well, it'll have to be in general terms ...

VIC It'll need to be ...

astride with one leg on each side, *G.* rittlings **barbed wire** wire with sharp points sticking out **to wince** to show pain or distress, *G.* zusammenzucken **to decline s.th.** *here:* to refuse to accept s.th. offered **three-handed** consisting of three people

TRUDY Excuse me, but why are you going back seventeen years? I mean, if you're talking about Vic's career, that only started eight years ago.

VIC It started the day I met you, my love …

Vic winks at Douglas again.

TRUDY (*unamused*) No, I mean it. Why are you wanting to go back seventeen years? I don't see any reason to.

JILL Because – (*as if talking to a child*) That's the point of the programme, Trudy. That's the name of the series, *Their Paths Crossed*. And seventeen years ago, that's when their paths crossed. These two. Douglas and Vic.

TRUDY Yes, I know. I just don't see why you have to go back through all that again. All that business in the bank – the trial –

JILL We're not. Not really –

VIC We are certainly not. Let's get that clear.

TRUDY (*clearly upset*) I don't see any point in dragging all that up again. We've got the kids growing up. A new life. Why do you want to talk about it, for heaven's sake … ?

VIC (*sharply to her*) Trudy! Listen, we're not going to talk about it, all right? (*Pause.*) Look, I think, actually, Trudy, in this instance, is right. We don't need to go back seventeen years, do we?

TRUDY No, we don't.

VIC It's pointless. I mean, I was inside for the first nine, so what's the point?

TRUDY There's no point.

JILL But seventeen years ago is when you met Mr Beechey. That's when your paths crossed. As a result of which, his life changed, your life changed.

VIC His life might have done. Mine didn't. I just went back to prison. That was nothing new to me then, I can tell you …

JILL Well, it certainly changed Mr Beechey's life –

VIC Well, do a programme about him, then. I don't mind.

JILL No, listen –

KENNY Vic, I think what Jill's saying is that that's the point of the programme. I mean, unless you do trace back to when you both met –

VIC No. Bugger it. I don't want to go back that far. Trudy's right. What's the point?

to drag s.th. up to rake up, *G.* (eine alte Geschichte) ausgraben **inside** *here:* in prison **to trace (s.th.) back to** to find out about s.th. by going back to its origins

TRUDY No point at all.

VIC Anyway, it's all in my book. If you want it, it's all there in the book.

TRUDY It wouldn't have been in that, either, if I'd had my way.

JILL (*trying to control her anger*) Well, terrific. (*Pause.*) You're not prepared to talk about the bank raid at all, then?

VIC Sorry, no. It's been done to death.

JILL Not like this it hasn't. (*Pause. Jill can see her programme disappearing.*) Not even in general detail?

VIC What do you mean, in general detail?

JILL I mean, just a general description of what happened. In very general terms. Look, I do appreciate that it isn't easy for either of you –

No one speaks.

I don't intend to go into any great lurid details. I was just planning to have both your voices speaking over a simple reconstruction – using posed actors in still pictures – I must stress that – I'm using stills, not even live action – I don't want anything sensational – God forbid – it's not a sensational slot, it can't be, it's scheduled for eight o'clock. That's all there would be. Just your voices over still pictures. Telling it as you remembered it. (*She stops and looks at them, awaiting response.*) I mean, none of what I'm saying is exactly new, you know. I did say all this to you, Kenneth. Originally. Months ago. Last November. Didn't I?

KENNY (*vaguely*) Yes. I know, it's just ... Obviously, if Vic feels ... (*He tails off.*)

VIC (*indicating Douglas*) Does he want to talk about this? You want all this dragged up again, Doug?

DOUGLAS Well ... I can see both points of view, really –

JILL Listen, the bulk of the programme, 99.999 per cent of it – I promise – is about what happened afterwards. About how you became a TV personality with an umpteen-million viewing figure –

KENNY Nine million.

raid *here:* robbery, hold-up **lurid** (*derog*) shocking, unnatural **to speak over (a scene)** (*TV*) to speak a commentary without appearing on the screen **posed** arranged in poses **still (picture)** non-moving picture, e.g. a photograph included in a film **scheduled for** to be shown at **to tail off** to become quiet **the bulk of** most, the greater part of **umpteen** (*infml*) indefinite but large number

Vic (*to Kenny*) Are we down to nine? Since when are we down to nine?

Vic Only for last week.

Vic Why?

Kenny Motor show.

Vic Oh.

Jill (*sensing a victory*) I think one of the fascinating things is the way both your careers have reversed, in a sense. I mean, seventeen years ago, Mr Beechey here was a national hero. Just looking at these press cuttings … (*She opens her folder.*) One newspaper actually started the Beechey Awards – given annually to anyone having a go at criminals. Isn't that right?

Douglas Yes, they did. I presented them myself the first year. At the Grosvenor House. A very splendid do.

Jill (*rifling through the cuttings*) 'Get that Beechey spirit, Britain' … 'We will fight them on the Beecheys' … 'Beechey's the boy for us'. (*examining a press photograph*) Who are all these women with you, incidentally?

Douglas Do you know, I never really found out. They just turned up in a coach one morning. With the photographer. We all got very chilly, I recall. Especially them.

Vic (*examining the cutting*) Dear, oh dear. (*showing it to Trudy*) Look at that … Disgraceful. (*He tuts with mock horror.*)

Jill But, looking at all these press cuttings, I wonder who'd remember you now?

Douglas Oh, no one at all, I shouldn't think.

Jill So heroes do get forgotten?

Douglas I think ones like me do.

Kenny (*studying one of the cuttings*) How long did they keep up these Beechey Awards?

Douglas Oh, three years. Then the paper went on to something else. Raising money for the Olympic Games, I think.

Jill Rather sad, don't you think?

to reverse to go in the opposite direction **press cutting** press clipping **award** prize **to have a go at s.b.** to attack s.b. **to present (an award)** to hand over officially **the Grosvenor House** name of a famous high-class hotel in London **a do** (*infml, BrE*) a big party, celebration **to rifle through** to go through quickly **"on the Beecheys"** play on words, cf. "on the beaches", i.e. of Normandy, where the Allied forces landed in 1944 to end the war **incidentally** by the way **to tut** to make a noise of disapproval with one's tongue

VIC No, that's life. Human nature. I mean, for the public, it's on to the next, isn't it? Has to be. Only natural.

JILL Only this particular hero was eventually to be replaced by the very man he so gallantly risked his life having a go at in the first place. A man who had fired a shotgun into an innocent girl's face –

TRUDY Listen, if we're going to start on that –

VIC (*sharply*) Trudy, sit down …

Trudy sits. Silence.

(*quietly*) Now that is an oversimplified statement and out of order, Jill. And you know it. Now, I'm prepared to do your interview – I've said I would, so I will – I'm prepared to do all I can to help you with your programme – but not if we're going to have semi-libellous statements chucked about the place, all right?

JILL I don't see your objections. Everybody knows you shot her. As you say, it's in your book. So what's the mystery?

TRUDY Because we're trying to forget it –

JILL If he's trying to forget it, why is he making money writing books about it?

KENNY No, that's totally unfair –

VIC Ten per cent of all my royalties from that book are going to recognized children charities –

JILL (*riding over this*) Why's he got a kids' programme on television and a chat show at weekends?

KENNY Because, put at its simplest, Vic has a personality which the public at large warm to and want to watch –

JILL They watch him because he used to be a bank robber. That's why they watch him.

KENNY That's total and complete bollocks – excuse me – none of the kids who watch Vic have the faintest idea what he used to be –

JILL Yes, they have –

KENNY They weren't even born –

shotgun a gun firing a great many tiny metal-balls, to kill birds **out of order** irregular **semi-** half-, near- **libellous** (*law*) untruthful and unfair **to chuck s.th.** (*infml*) to throw s.th. **royalties** income from books or music paid by the publisher to the author **a charity** a non-profit-making organization helping people in need **bollocks** (*taboo sl*) nonsense

JILL Yes, they have because he tells them. Listen to me, kids, I went down the wrong street once and believe me, tangling with the law is strictly for mugs –

VIC Now, hold on. Hold on. Be fair –

KENNY Do you realize the number of kids this man has kept out of prison ... ?

JILL I've no doubt he has –

KENNY There have been surveys done amongst underprivileged kids –

JILL I'm sure. I'm not saying Vic isn't doing a wonderful job. He is. Of course he is. All I'm saying is – all I'm saying – (*She hesitates.*)

TRUDY (*coolly*) What exactly are you saying? Exactly?

JILL All I'm saying is – isn't it ironic that the hero is forgotten? And the villain has now become the hero. That's all. And isn't that a reflection of our time?

TRUDY Fascinating.

JILL And whilst we're saying it, isn't it even more tragic that the person who lost most in all this – the victim herself – no one spares a thought for her at all. Except Douglas, of course.

TRUDY (*muttering*) I knew we'd get round to this ...

VIC If you think I didn't spend nine years of my life thinking about that girl, then you don't know me – that's all I can say. I have woken in the night – (*to Trudy*) I still do occasionally – don't I? In a sweat, wringing wet, still remembering it. So don't you come at me with that one. I paid –

TRUDY Vic –

VIC No, let me finish – I paid the full penalty as prescribed by the law for what I did. In full. Fourteen years less remission – nine years. And that to me has to mean a debt paid in full. Otherwise what more can a man do? Eh? Go on blaming himself? What's the point of that?

TRUDY No point.

VIC None. He has got to get up and do the very best with that which God has granted him to make amends with and try and put something back in the world, in the brief time left to him.

to tangle with s.b./s.th. to get involved, to quarrel with s.b./s.th. **mug** (*infml*) stupid person **to hesitate** to pause before doing, or going on with **to mutter** to speak in a low and angry voice **to wring** to twist wet clothes so that water is removed **penalty** punishment **remission** (*law*) reduction of punishment because of good behaviour **to make amends** to compensate (for a wrong one has done)

And that is what, hand on heart, I have tried to do. Bear me out, Kenny, is that not what I have tried to do … ?

KENNY Absolutely, Vic.

VIC Right. (*to Jill*) Jill, there is no use in going back over the past where no one is going to benefit. It's not going to help me. (*indicating Douglas*) It's not going to help him. And it's certainly not going to help that poor bloody bitch who was injured – sorry, she's your wife, mate, I shouldn't refer to her like that … It's not going to help her either …

TRUDY Not in the least.

KENNY Absolutely not.

Pause.

VIC I mean, you talk about villains, you talk about heroes. But what is that? It's very often a value judgement made by society, which has no basis in fact whatsoever. I mean, has it?

JILL I don't know. You tell me.

VIC Well, I'm telling you. It hasn't. I mean, take that instance. I'm cast as the villain, right? Because it just so happens that on that particular occasion it was me who happened to be the one who walked into the bank with a shotgun with the intention of robbing it. Another day, another time, another set of circumstances, it could have been someone else, couldn't it? Could have been you. Could have been him. Now, I'm not pretending that what I did was a right course of action – But. But, let's add these factors. I had no intention at any stage of using that firearm. It was on my previous record for all to see that I never used a firearm, I never condoned the use of firearms. I detest firearms. Even now – Well, we did a programme on firearms the other day, didn't we, Kenny? Kenny here will vouch for me, I couldn't even bring myself to pick one up, could I? And if you will care to check, and it is on record from sworn witnesses at the trial, the very first words I said when the three of us first came through those bank doors, my first words were: 'All right. Don't get excited and nobody'll get injured.' (*to Douglas*) You were there. Did I not say those exact words?

to bear s.b. out to confirm as true what s.b. has said **bitch** (*derog.*) spiteful woman **mate** (*infml*) friend, colleague **to cast s.b.** (*theatre*) to give s.b. a certain role **circumstance** detail, fact, condition **previous record** (*law*) written report of a criminal's past **to condone s.th.** to approve of, to tolerate s.th. **to detest s.b./s.th.** to dislike s.b./s.th. very much **to vouch for s.b.** to declare one's firm belief in s.b.

DOUGLAS Nobody'll get hurt. Don't get excited and nobody'll get hurt, you said ...

VIC There you are. Would I have said that if I'd come in there to shoot somebody?

JILL But the gun was loaded –

VIC Well, yes, it was loaded. What's the point of carrying an empty gun?

JILL So you knew you might use it?

VIC (*sharply*) I've said I had no intention of using it, all right? Is my word not good enough?

A pause.

DOUGLAS The safety catch was off, though.

VIC (*irritably*) What?

DOUGLAS I said, the safety catch was off. I remember the police saying so at the time.

VIC Well, of course it was. Look, come on, be fair. You cannot walk into a bank with a gun and expect people to take you seriously if you've still got the safety on, can you?

JILL Why not?

VIC (*angrily*) Because people aren't going to take much notice of you for a kick off, are they? All they're going to say is, this geezer's an idiot, he's wandering round with his safety on ...

JILL Most people would never know the difference, would they? I wouldn't know if a safety catch was on or off.

VIC Maybe you wouldn't. But some people would, that's all I'm saying ...

JILL You mean other bank robbers?

VIC Look, there's plenty of people besides bank robbers who use shotguns, you know. I mean, a lot of people use shotguns. People working in the bank, they probably use shotguns –

JILL What, in the bank?

VIC At the weekend. They probably use shotguns.

JILL Do you use one?

DOUGLAS No, I never use shotguns.

VIC Not him. I'm not talking about him. I mean, the managers. As a matter of fact, I think my manager shoots. (*to Kenny*) David shoots, doesn't he? David?

safety catch a kind of lock to stop a gun from being fired **irritably** (*adv*) angrily
for a kick off (*infml*) for a start **geezer** (*infml*) funny, strange man

KENNY No, I think he water-skis.

VIC No. Well, there are some. Take my word for it. Anyway, the point I am making is, responsible as I may have been – and I've never denied that – for carrying a gun into that place (*indicating Douglas*), if this one hadn't come at me – if this six-and-a-half-stone boy-scout bank clerk hadn't come charging at me from the length of the bank – I would never have fired –

JILL You're not saying it was Mr Beechey's fault, are you?

VIC No. I'm not saying that. But if he hadn't been a hero, if he hadn't grabbed me, the gun would never have gone off accidentally and this girl would never have got hurt. I mean, as it was, he was clinging on – I was shouting – 'Be careful, it'll go off, it'll go off' – and I could see, you know, this girl was in the firing line –

JILL She was the one you'd been holding as a hostage?

VIC Yes, originally. But I'd released her in order to wrestle with him. As soon as I appreciated the danger, I let her go. I could see, though, as he and I were struggling, that the gun was twisting round towards her – (*to Douglas*) You had your back to her, so you couldn't have seen – and I was trying, you know, to pull it back away from her – and then, before I can do anything to stop it, bang – Right in the side of her face. It was a miracle, with the gun that close, she didn't lose an eye. A miracle. I thank God for that, at least.

A respectful pause.

DOUGLAS She did lose her ear, though.

VIC Well, yes. Still. An ear's not the same as eye, is it?

KENNY I suppose she could grow her hair …

DOUGLAS Yes, she did.

VIC She's all right now, then, is she?

DOUGLAS Oh, yes. She's pretty chirpy. Has her ups and downs, of course.

TRUDY Like most of us.

VIC Lovely girl.

stone traditional British weight, 6.350 kg, so Douglas's weight is given as only 41.28 kg! **accidentally** (*adv*) by mistake **hostage** a person held as a prisoner **to release** to allow (a prisoner) to go away

DOUGLAS Yes, she was.

KENNY Lucky man.

DOUGLAS Yes, she was beautiful.

JILL She still is. From what I saw of her, anyway.

VIC She's not in the film?

JILL No.

DOUGLAS I think she'd have found it difficult –

VIC Oh, yes.

JILL And, anyway, as I keep saying, this programme is really about you two. Not her at all. I don't want it to be macabre or morbid or cause a lot of unnecessary pain – I mean, frankly, I'm not into that sort of programme, I'm sorry. I mean, I know some people make careers out of it, we've all seen them, they love to have the camera lingering over people crying and obviously in terrible distress, but I'm sorry, I find that simply gratuitous and tasteless. That's not what I'm here to do. And if that means I'm into old-fashioned programme values, then you'll have to forgive me.

VIC Hear! Hear! You and me both, baby. (*Pause.*) So is that it, then? Are we excused? Only I think I fancy a swim.

TRUDY Just a minute. Have you agreed to talk about the robbery or not?

JILL Only very, very, very briefly. I need to a little, just to establish the programme.

TRUDY Well, it had better be briefly.

VIC It'll be brief, don't worry. It's old news, anyway. Who's interested? (*indicating Douglas*) He doesn't want it dragged up, I don't want it dragged up. His wife certainly doesn't. So that's the end of it. You fancy a swim, Doug?

DOUGLAS Er, no …

VIC Before we have a drink …

DOUGLAS No, me and water, I'm afraid, I –

TRUDY (*in sudden alarm*) Timmy! (*Trudy rushes off to the far end of the swimming pool.*) Cindy, hold on to him!

Vic moves towards the pool after Trudy.

JILL (*seeing what's happening*) Oh, my God.

morbid (*derog*) fascinated by death **to be into s.th.** (*infml*) to be interested in s.th. **distress** grief, suffering **gratuitous** [grə'tju:ɪtəs] unnecessary, not justified **to fancy s.b./s.th.** (*infml*) to like, to wish for s.b./s.th.

VIC Have you got him?

TRUDY (*off*) You naughty boy. Don't ever do that again. (*calling*) Yes, he's all right. My God, he nearly went in. (*to Timmy*) Now, I told you before ...

Jill, Kenny and Douglas have risen to watch.

KENNY That was a close thing.

JILL He's all right, though.

DOUGLAS Could have been nasty –

Sharon appears from the house. She has changed into her swimsuit. She stops to watch the commotion.

SHARON What's happening?

JILL Timmy nearly fell in. Weren't you supposed to be keeping an eye on them?

SHARON I just went to change – (*calling*) Is he all right?

Vic turns from the pool and looks at Sharon.

VIC (*beckoning Sharon*) Hey, come here.

SHARON What?

VIC Here. Come here.

Sharon crosses obediently over to him. Vic speaks to her quietly, but not so quietly that the others cannot hear him.

Where the bloody hell have you been, eh?

SHARON Pardon, Mr Parks ...

VIC (*very close to her*) My kid was practically drowned, and where were you? Eh?

SHARON (*frightened*) I was changing, Mr Parks ...

VIC Changing? I see. You were changing while my child was nearly drowning. That's your idea of looking after them, is it? Is it?

SHARON (*with a reflex smile due to pure nervousness*) No.

VIC I hope you're not laughing about this, girl, because I'm not. Are you laughing? It's a joke to you, is it? Is it a joke?

Sharon can't reply. She shakes her head.

commotion excitement, exciting scene or activity **to beckon s.b.** to call s.b. by a movement of the body

Do you hear what I'm saying to you? I'm asking you, do you think it's a joke? Do you?

JILL Vic ...

VIC I'm waiting to hear from you. Do you think it's a joke?

SHARON No, Mr Parks.

VIC Good. I'm delighted to hear that. Because if you had done, you'd have been on the next plane straight out of here, all right? Straight back to Macclesfield, all right?

SHARON Yes, Mr Parks.

VIC And in the meantime, did you not come equipped with a uniform? Eh?

SHARON Sorry?

VIC I said, did you not have a uniform when you arrived here?

SHARON Yes, Mr Parks.

VIC Then, in future, when you are on duty will you kindly wear it, as you're supposed to do.

SHARON Yes, Mr Parks.

VIC Is that understood?

SHARON Yes, Mr Parks.

VIC Then get upstairs and get changed. You look disgusting dressed like that, anyway.

Sharon rushes off, starting to cry as she goes. Vic glares after her.

Bloody girl. Do you know how much we're paying for her?

JILL It's all right, Vic, the kids are fine. Look, they're playing again. They soon forget.

VIC All right then. Time for a swim. (*calling to the other end of the pool*) Look out, you two. Here comes a crocodile ...

Vic goes off to the end of the pool, throwing aside his shirt as he goes. In a second, we hear the diving board vibrate and then a splash as he dives in.

JILL Well, I suppose I'd better go and find my film crew. Wake them up.

DOUGLAS Well. I'm ready when you are, Jill.

JILL (*drily*) Thank you, Mr Beechey. That's most reassuring.

to be equipped with to have as part of one's clothes, tools etc. **to glare** to look angrily **to reassure s.b.** to stop s.b. from worrying

She goes out through the garden gate. Throughout the next, Vic will occasionally appear at this end of the pool. He is evidently swimming length after length. Douglas and Kenny watch him idly. Vic turns and swims away.

KENNY (*at length*) You know, there's only one thing about that story of Vic's – I mean, it's not the first time I've heard it, naturally – but I've always wondered, why on earth did you do such a bean-brained thing like that? I mean, running straight at a man who's armed with a loaded shotgun? What on earth made you do it?

DOUGLAS Do you know, I've often asked myself that and I haven't the faintest idea.

KENNY Do you make a habit of that sort of thing? Sudden reckless gestures? I mean, do you mountaineer, jump out of aeroplanes? Things like that?

DOUGLAS No. Certainly not.

KENNY Extraordinary. I don't know about making you a hero. You were lucky not to have been locked up as a lunatic.

Vic appears momentarily at this end of the pool. He turns and swims back out of view.

DOUGLAS Well, funnily enough, that's exactly what the police said to me at the time. They called it a very foolhardy, reckless gesture.

KENNY They still made a hero of you.

DOUGLAS I don't think the police did that. That was the press. They said I'd captured the general public's imagination.

KENNY No problem. That's about as easy to capture as a dead chicken in a meat safe. Gallant bank clerk risks life to save fiancée?

DOUGLAS So the story went. Actually, Nerys wasn't even my fiancée. Not at the time.

KENNY No? I always understood she was.

at length after some time, at last **bean** (*infml*) the smallest quantity or size **to mountaineer** to climb on mountains **reckless** hasty, without thinking of possible consequences **lunatic** madman, crazy person **foolhardy** foolishly spontaneous and dangerous **to capture s.th.** to catch s.th. **meat safe** cupboard for keeping meat **gallant** (*fml*) courageous **fiancé/-ée** man/woman to whom one is engaged

DOUGLAS No, she was actually engaged to someone else when it happened, but – after the – accident – he – her fiancé – broke it off. And this reporter said it would be an altogether better story if he could say that Nerys and I were engaged. And I said it would probably be all right. And he said, well, when she'd regained consciousness, if subsequently we both went off the idea and decided to split up again, that would make another good story.

Vic appears briefly again.

KENNY Ah. (*He considers this.*) I see. Well, I think I'll have a dip. Expose the alabaster limbs. Just go and root out some trunks. You're not swimming?

DOUGLAS No. If it's all the same.

KENNY It's all the same to me, chum.

Kenny saunters into the house. As he does so, he passes Marta, who comes out of the house and starts, unsmilingly, to clear the coffee things.

DOUGLAS Very nice cup of coffee. Thank you. *Gracias.*

Marta ignores him. Douglas wanders around and explores the place a little. The children's shouts are heard, happy again. The distant splash of water. A plane flies over, Douglas shields his eyes and watches it pass. Vic appears once more.

VIC (*as he turns, spluttering*) 'S great. You want to try it.

He swims away. Trudy returns from the far end of the pool.

TRUDY (*calling to the children*) You stay that end. Stay up that end, do you hear? Keep an eye on them, won't you, Vic?

Vic's spluttered reply is heard.

(*to Douglas*) Sure you don't want a swim?

DOUGLAS No, I –

TRUDY It's lovely and warm ...

subsequently (*adv*) following this, later **to have a dip** (*infml*) to go for a short swim **to root out s.th.** to search and find s.th. **to saunter** to walk slowly **to splutter** to talk while spitting out water

DOUGLAS No, I – always look a little foolish in the water.

TRUDY Oh, I'm sure you look fine ... You should see me. These days. I'm no bathing beauty ...

DOUGLAS (*gallantly*) Oh, come now ...

TRUDY Nobody'll see you. Not here.

DOUGLAS It's very peaceful. Quite a contrast. When I left first thing this morning it was pouring with rain.

TRUDY Ah ...

DOUGLAS Forty-three degrees.

TRUDY Yes?

DOUGLAS Fahrenheit.

TRUDY Yes.

DOUGLAS I can never work out the other one, I'm afraid.

TRUDY No?

DOUGLAS That's a terrible admission for someone working in double glazing.

He laughs. Trudy smiles. Vic appears briefly in the pool again. They watch him.

He's a good swimmer, Vic.

TRUDY Yes, he's very good. Mind you, he can do most things. Once he sets his mind to them. I've always said if Vic can't do something, then it's probably only because he doesn't want to do it in the first place.

She pauses as Sharon comes out of the house. She is now dressed in her nursemaid's uniform – a little incongruously considering the temperature.

Why on earth are you dressed up like that, Sharon? It's sweltering.

SHARON (*sulkily*) Mr Parks said I had to.

TRUDY Really? Oh, well. If Mr Parks told you to ...

SHARON (*aloof*) Excuse me, please.

She marches off towards the pool. Trudy stares at her sourly.

DOUGLAS He certainly tore her off a strip just now, your husband.

TRUDY Did he?

nursemaid a trained young woman looking after little children, nanny **incongruously** (*adv*) out of place **sweltering** extremely hot and moist **aloof** reserved, unfriendly **to tear s.b. off a strip** (*infml*) to criticize s.b. in a very unfriendly, tactless way

DOUGLAS I wouldn't have cared to have been on the receiving end of that.

TRUDY Don't worry. It always looks worse than it is.

DOUGLAS Does he do that a lot, then?

TRUDY Oh, yes. Quite a lot. It's not quite as it appears.

Vic appears again briefly.

Vic often shouts at women.

DOUGLAS (*laughing uncertainly*) I hope not at you.

TRUDY He's like a lot of men I've met. They don't quite know what to do with a woman when they've got her, so they shout at her.

DOUGLAS I don't think I've ever shouted at Nerys ...

TRUDY No, well, you're probably different. Perhaps you're one of those men who do know what to do with a woman once you've got her ...

DOUGLAS (*laughing self-consciously*) I don't – quite know what to say to that. (*He laughs again.*) I hope I do. (*He laughs.*) I've got a pretty fair idea, yes. (*Pause. Suddenly feeling the heat*) It's going to be a scorcher, isn't it? A real scorcher.

TRUDY Would you like to take your jacket off?

DOUGLAS Er ...

TRUDY And your – pullover. You must be very hot.

DOUGLAS Well, I think, with your permission – the jacket, thank you ...

He removes his jacket. Trudy takes it from him and hangs it on a chair. As this is happening, Vic appears again briefly.

Thank you.

TRUDY I'm sorry, I really am.

DOUGLAS Sorry?

TRUDY I mean, it must be obvious that I didn't want you to come here – I didn't want to meet you and I didn't want Vic to meet you again. I still don't know why he agreed to it. I suppose Jill must have ... If you'd brought your wife with you – I don't know what I'd have done. Probably run away, I think.

DOUGLAS There would have been no need for that, I'm sure.

self-consciously (*adv*) embarrassed, nervous, unsure of oneself **scorcher** extremely hot day

TRUDY I think you're amazing, I really do. When you think of what happened to her – and to you – and then you willingly come here and see us with – all this – Amazing. (*She laughs. Pause.*) Of course, being only human, it keeps occurring to me that maybe you want something from us. And maybe you haven't yet said what it is.

DOUGLAS Is that how I appear to be?

TRUDY No, you don't. Not at all. But one can't help wondering, none the less. Being only human. (*Pause.*) I don't know if there is anything we can do. I can do. Anything we can give you. Or offer you. But if there is … I mean it. Anything. Take it. Please. Take it.

She looks at Douglas. He looks at her.

DOUGLAS (*gently*) No. Really. There's nothing you have that I could possibly take. Thank you all the same.

Trudy nods and goes into the house. Douglas looks about him once more. Then sits on a sun lounger. Cindy, the child, runs on from the pool. She is in her swimming costume and her wet feet leave a trail across the patio. She has a very soggy bunch of wild grasses and weeds. A child's bouquet. She stands in front of Douglas and holds them out to him.

Are these for me?

Cindy nods.

(*taking the offering from her*) Thank you very much. How lovely …

Cindy rushes away to the pool again.

(*as she disappears*) Thank you.

Douglas stands holding the bouquet. He looks around him. Then at the bouquet. The sound of splashing and Vic now playing with the happy children at the other end of the pool. Douglas continues to stand looking around. There is an expression on his face that could just be the start of a growing envy. Jill, quite suddenly and purposefully, walks out from the house, into the centre of the patio.

soggy damp and shapeless **purposefully** (*adv*) determined

JILL (*shouting to the invisible film crew*) And cut.

The voices from the pool and the splashing stop abruptly.

Thank you. Thank you, Douglas.

DOUGLAS Was that all right?

JILL Perfect. Thank you. (*to the crew*) Keep that set up, we've just got time to do their first meeting before lunch.

Shouts from the crew.

Yes, we can. We've got nearly fifteen minutes. Douglas, I want to do yours and Vic's meeting first, all right?

DOUGLAS (*putting down his bouquet*) Right-oh, yes.

Jill is arranging three of the upright chairs into a loose semicircular 'interview' set-up. Douglas puts on his jacket again. A distant call from the crew.

JILL (*in response*) Why not?

Distant technical explanation.

Well, too bloody bad ... Dan, I'm replugging now. This will be a mute sequence. It's just so I can talk to you. All right?

As she fiddles to reconnect her radio mic, Vic enters from the house. He has now changed and is spruced up for TV – a casual, manly image: blazer, lightweight tropical trousers, sunglasses and just the right number of shirt buttons undone.

VIC What's going on?

JILL I just want to do the first meeting with Mr Beechey, Vic – if you don't mind ... The one we didn't get earlier.

VIC Nearly lunchtime, isn't it?

JILL No, we've got (*consulting her watch*) – twelve and a half minutes – I literally just want the two of you meeting, OK? Very simple. All in long. No sound. If I can get the establishing shot now, then we'll start the interviews after lunch. Douglas, my love ...

to fiddle to use one's fingers nervously **spruced-up** (*infml*) smartly dressed **casual** (esp. of clothes) informal **in long** (*TV, referring to camera position*) long-distance shot **establishing shot** (*TV*) the shot showing the whole of the set in context

DOUGLAS Hallo.

JILL OK. Listen, I want you simply to come in through that gate – like this – (*she demonstrates*) OK?

DOUGLAS (*watching her intently*) Yes. I came in the other way, originally. When I arrived. Does that matter?

JILL Not in the least.

VIC This is television. It's all fiction, son. All fiction. (*He winks at Douglas.*)

JILL (*slightly coolly*) Not all of it. But in this case it doesn't matter. (*demonstrating*) Now, I want you to walk to the middle of the patio – like this – stop – look around you – never seen anywhere like it in your life – gasp, gasp – and then we'll see Vic coming out from the house to greet you. OK?

DOUGLAS Yes, yes ...

VIC You want me from the house?

JILL Please.

VIC As soon as he stops?

JILL Yes. I can talk you through it. It'll be with voice-over this, eventually. I just want you both to meet, apparently start talking for a second or two, and then I'll come out and join you – and we'll sit – here – (*She indicates the three chairs, then into her mic.*) Are you getting all this, Dan? I hope you are, and can you relay it to George? Douglas, can you sit this side – here? (*She indicates one of the side chairs.*)

DOUGLAS There. Right.

JILL And Vic, you'll sit here. OK?

VIC OK.

JILL Then I can be between you. All right, shall we have a quick run first? Can you both take your places. Douglas, just outside the gate.

Douglas hurries back to wait outside the gate, ever cooperative. Vic strolls back into the house in a rather more leisurely manner.

(*into her mic*) Dan, will you tell George we'll do it once so he can look at it. OK?

She looks in the crew's direction. A shout from them.

voice-over (*TV*) commentary spoken by invisible speaker **to indicate s.b./s.th.** to point to s.b./s.th.

OK, this is just a rehearsal and – action. Thank you, Douglas. (*She steps back into the house doorway.*) Douglas … Come on, please …

Douglas sticks his head round the gate.

DOUGLAS All right?

JILL Yes, come on. Come on. Keep walking in …

Douglas walks in through the gate. He has a lot of trouble walking to order. His arms and legs are rather uncoordinated.

Come on in further, Douglas. And try not to look at the camera if you can help it …

DOUGLAS (*trying not to move his lips*) Sorry.

JILL Relax, try and relax. Douglas. Act normally …

DOUGLAS Yes, I'm trying to act normally …

JILL Now, look around you … you haven't seen this place before, have you?

DOUGLAS No.

JILL Look around then. Take it all in.

DOUGLAS (*looking round, still speaking like an unsuccessful ventriloquist*) Yes, I'm taking it in, yes …

JILL Well, look a bit amazed – look a little awed by it all –

Douglas tries to look awed.

More. More. Isn't it an amazing place, Douglas? You've never seen anything like it in your life …

Douglas tries to look awed.

Talk if you want to. You can talk if you feel like it …

DOUGLAS (*looking around*) Sorry. There doesn't seem to be anyone here to talk to –

JILL (*muttering, despairingly*) Oh, Jesus … Thank you, and cue Vic …

Vic strides out from the house, hand extended.

to order (*adv*) following instructions **ventriloquist** a person speaking with apparently closed lips, *G.* Bauchredner **amazed** deeply impressed **awed** feeling respect combined with fear or wonder **cue** (*theatre*) the sign for an actor to walk onto the stage **to stride** to take long steps **extended** stretched out, offered for a handshake

VIC (*to Douglas, genially*) Hallo ...

DOUGLAS (*equally genial, shaking Vic's hand*) Oh, hallo, there.

VIC Hallo.

DOUGLAS Hallo.

Pause.

VIC (*laughing*) That's about all I have to say to you.

JILL Keep talking, please. Just a bit more.

VIC You must be the man come to deliver the coal?

DOUGLAS Pardon? (*getting the joke*) Oh, yes. Right. I've got it in the van out there.

VIC Oh, good. You sold your handcart, I take it?

DOUGLAS Yes, oh, yes. I sold my handcart. Got fifty pesetas for it.

He laughs at his own inventiveness. Jill emerges from the doorway to join them both.

JILL Yes, OK, something like that. And then I'll say, hallo, sorry to interrupt – this might be quite a strange feeling for you both, meeting after – what is it – seventeen years?

DOUGLAS Yes, seventeen.

VIC Is it seventeen? Good gracious me.

JILL And then I'll say something else and then I'll suggest we all sit down, shall we? (*She indicates the three chairs.*)

VIC What a charming idea!

DOUGLAS Why not? Take the weight off the feet after my long journey. Phew!

VIC Good flight was it? Anyone fall out?

DOUGLAS Wonderful flight. British Airways. You can't beat them. Not for flying.

Vic has sat down in his designated seat. Douglas, carried away by the improvised conversation, has seated himself in the middle chair.

JILL (*irritated by all this badinage*) No, Douglas. Douglas ...

VIC I think you're meant to be in that one, Mr Coalman.

JILL This one, please ... That's mine.

genially (*adv*) friendly and cheerful **inventiveness** ability to invent s.th. **good gracious me** exclamation of surprise **to designate** to name, to choose **badinage** (*fml*) humorous talk, joking

DOUGLAS Oh, I am sorry. I beg your pardon. Carried away. I really enjoy filming, you know. I didn't think I would. I think I could even enjoy it as a career.

Douglas sits in his correct seat, as he speaks. Jill sits in hers.

JILL OK. Then as soon as we're settled here, I'll cut. And we'll pick it up after lunch for close-ups in these same positions, OK?

DOUGLAS Yes, yes ... That sounds a good plan.

JILL All right, Dan? That work all right for George?

A distant shout.

What?

The shout is repeated.

Yes, I know, I told him that. (*to Douglas*) They're saying, can you try not to notice the camera?

DOUGLAS Yes, I'm sorry, I'm sorry ...

VIC Try and defocus your eyes, that's the tip – otherwise it's very difficult not to look at it – The camera's like a magnet, you know what I mean ... ?

DOUGLAS Yes, yes, thank you ...

VIC Defocus ... That's what I do. That's the way to do it.

DOUGLAS Thank you very much, I'll try that.

JILL (*who has been looking off towards the camera crew*) OK. Here we go for real this time. Places again, please. We're very short of time.

Vic goes back into the house. Douglas starts for the gate but is called back by Jill.

Douglas –

DOUGLAS Yes, Jill.

JILL Just – when you meet Vic this time ... I don't think you want to be – what shall I say – quite so overjoyed to see him ...

DOUGLAS Oh, no, no, that was just ...

JILL I mean, here's a man you haven't seen for seventeen years and the last time you saw him he was firing a shotgun into the face of the woman you loved – so ...

to defocus one's eyes to avoid looking directly at any object or person **for real** (*adv*) seriously

DOUGLAS Yes, I see …

JILL I mean, it just looks odd – if you greet him like a long-lost brother. I think – you know – just a little wariness and a sense that perhaps you haven't *quite* forgiven and forgotten – I mean, I know maybe you have – but it would certainly look more natural – to the average viewer … Do you follow?

DOUGLAS Yes. Yes. No, it was only …

A yell from the crew.

JILL (*in response to this*) Yes, OK, OK. We have to get on. We've got five minutes. Can you try and give me all that?

DOUGLAS Yes, I'll try. I'll try.

JILL Bless you. Thank you, Douglas … Thank you very, very deeply.

Douglas goes off through the gate.

All right, everyone. (*into her mic*) Tell George to yell as soon as he's rolling … (*A pause.*) Stand by, everyone. One take. That's all we've got.

Slight pause. A distant shout.

OK. And – action! (*as she retreats right into the house this time*) Thank you, Douglas.

A slight pause. Douglas enters through the gate. His eyes are defocused, so he is tending to peer around a little myopically, his eyes screwed up.

(*muttering*) What the hell's he doing, he looks like Mr Magoo … (*calling*) That's lovely, Douglas. Keep going. Try and look up a little. Look around the place as you come in … Oh, no!

Ruy has entered by the pool with a hosepipe in his hand. He stops by the edge and watches the proceedings. An ironic cheer from the crew, who are evidently well away.

All right. Keep rolling. Keep rolling. Keep going, Douglas. (*hissing to Ruy*) Back! Back! Piss off!

wariness being reserved and watchful **to peer** to look hard without seeing clearly **myopic(ally)** short-sighted **screwed up** half closed from the effort of looking **hosepipe** a long flexible tube made of rubber, used to water the garden **evidently** (*adv*) obviously **to hiss** to make a long "s"-sound, *G.* zischen **piss off** (*sl*) go away

Ruy appears not to notice her.

(*into her mic*) Dan! Dan! Can you hear me? Don't let that man wander into shot. Someone get that sodding gardener out of shot. (*calling*) Super, Douglas. Perfect. Now, stop there and look around you. Just don't look at the gardener, he's not really there.

Someone, unseen, flicks the other end of Ruy's hosepipe to try to attract his attention. Ruy fails to notice, so engrossed is he in watching Douglas, who is staring about him myopically.

Come on, Douglas, give us a bit of surprise. (*hissing angrily into her mic again*) Will somebody get rid of that bloody gardener ...

Douglas tries to look surprised. Ruy's hosepipe twitches again, rather more violently. He gives it a passing glance but continues to hold on to it, watching intently.

Come on, Douglas, real amazement now – (*furiously into mic*) Get that half-wit out of shot! All the amazement you can muster now, Douglas.

Douglas is staring about him open-mouthed. As he looks at Ruy, who is standing looking at Douglas, equally fascinated, someone gives the hosepipe a really fierce tug. Ruy is pulled off his feet, overbalances and with a cry falls backwards into the pool. Douglas looks genuinely alarmed.

DOUGLAS What happened?

JILL All right! Ignore that. He'll be OK. Carry on. We're desperately short of time. Cue Vic. Thank you, Vic.

Vic comes out of the house, genially, as before.

VIC Hallo ...

JILL Remember, suspicious of him, Douglas – suspicious.

DOUGLAS (*suspiciously*) Hallo, who are you?

shot (*TV*) area covered by the camera from its present position **sodding** (*taboo sl*) damned **to flick s.th.** to move s.th. lightly and quickly **engrossed** absorbed **to muster s.th.** (*fml*) to collect and show **fierce** very angry **tug** pull **suspicious of s.b.** not trusting s.b.

RUY (*bobbing up in the swimming pool*) Help!

Douglas turns to see if Ruy is all right.

JILL Douglas, keep looking at Vic. Remember who he is.

DOUGLAS Yes, sorry.

VIC Did you have a good flight?

DOUGLAS (*suspiciously*) What do you mean by that exactly?

RUY (*coming up again*) Help! Mr Vic!

DOUGLAS (*turning again*) Is he all right?

VIC (*genially, still*) No, I think he's drowning ...

JILL Keep chatting, I need more chat. Don't worry about the gardener, he's not in shot. Keep chatting together. Vic, point out the garden to Douglas ...

VIC (*obeying her*) Well, now. This is the patio ...

DOUGLAS Oh, yes ...

VIC You may have noticed it as you walked over it. And that's our swimming pool over there ...

DOUGLAS Lovely ...

JILL Super, that's super, chaps ...

RUY (*coming up again*) Help!

VIC And that's our gardener over there, coming up for the third time ...

JILL Keep talking, Douglas. Come on. Time is against us.

DOUGLAS (*worried*) Can he swim, do you think?

VIC I shouldn't imagine so. Not in those boots.

DOUGLAS Good Lord ...

RUY Help! Please! Mr Vic!

Jill moves out to join them as before.

JILL Hallo there, gentlemen, sorry to interrupt –

RUY Help!

JILL Vic, Douglas, this must be quite a strange feeling for both of you meeting after – what is it – seventeen years?

VIC Certainly is.

DOUGLAS I think we ought to do something.

RUY (*spluttering*) Aaarrgghh!

DOUGLAS I really think he's drowning, you know ...

JILL Douglas, how does it feel meeting after all this time?

to bob up to come to the surface suddenly

Douglas (*distracted by Ruy*) What? Oh, very nice, thank you very much. (*He smiles.*)

Jill (*fiercely*) Don't smile. (*pleasantly again*) Well, perhaps we should all sit down, should we?

Vic Good idea.

Douglas Why not?

Ruy Aaarrgghh!

They all go to sit. Douglas, distracted, again threatens to sit in the wrong chair.

Jill This chair, Douglas, this one, please.

Douglas Sorry.

Jill And chat, chat, chat, chat, chat ...

Vic Chat, chat, chat ...

Jill (*getting up again*) And that's it. Super. Thank you both.

Ruy (*spitting out water*) Ooooorrrggghh!

Jill moves towards where the crew are and talks into her mic.

Jill Dan, can you ask George if he managed to keep off that idiot? Did he manage to keep the gardener out of shot ... ? Ask him.

Vic moves to Ruy and starts to pull him, exhausted, from the water.

Vic Come on, you'll be all right. Come on, old lad.

Douglas stands watching, amazed.

You get off home and have your dinner. You'll feel better then ... You mustn't interrupt the filming, you know.

Ruy (*weakly*) No. Thank you, Mr Vic, thank you. Sorry. Sorry.

Vic There you go ...

Ruy (*staggering off along the poolside*) Sorry, Mr Vic ...

Vic OK. Don't worry about it, old son.

Ruy exits gasping and panting. A shout from the crew.

distracted unable to concentrate, worried **to exit** (*theatre*) to go off, leave the stage **to gasp** to breathe deeply and with difficulty, *G.* nach Luft schnappen **to pant** to breathe quickly and with difficulty, *G.* keuchen

JILL What? He did? Oh, terrific. (*to Vic and Douglas*) That's fine. George apparently managed to pan off the gardener and still keep the full patio in frame, so we're OK. That's great. Lunch-time, is it?

VIC One minute past one.

JILL Pretty good going.

VIC Want a drink first?

Jill looks doubtful.

Come on, just a little one.

JILL Well, a little one perhaps ...

VIC (*to Douglas*) Doug?

DOUGLAS Mmm?

VIC Coming in for lunch?

DOUGLAS (*still a little dazed*) Oh yes. Thank you. Yes.

They all move towards the house. Douglas stops to pick up his bouquet on the way.

JILL (*as they go*) God, you know, I had this dreadful fear that that man was going to be in shot through the entire sequence. I mean, the thought of having to set the whole thing up again after lunch ...

Vic steps aside to let Jill, then Douglas enter. Shouts are heard from the crew.

VIC (*returning to make out what they're saying*) What's that?

More shouts. Douglas and Jill come out again.

JILL What are they saying?

VIC Apparently you didn't say cut. They just want to know if you'd finished the shot.

JILL Well, obviously I've finished. Idiots. (*shouting*) Of course I've finished. (*loudly*) Cut!

A sudden blackout.

to pan (*techn*) to move the camera horizontally **in frame** (*techn*) in shot **dazed** confused, shocked

Act Two

Later that same afternoon. At the start, as before, there is just a light on Jill who sits on the patio doing a piece to camera. The film crew, as always, are out of sight.

JILL It became increasingly clear that the quiet, law-abiding, undemanding Douglas Beechey we had met and spoken to in Purley a few days before was a very different creature from the man who had arrived here at the Parks' villa earlier that day. Here was a person who, at last, seemed to have discovered a long-lost purpose. As each of his senses, in turn, took in the unfamiliar – the sweet perfume of luxury, the rich, clean vista of good living, the comfortable, self-confident murmur of opulence – his manner grew ever more watchful – increasingly thoughtful. Were these merely the signs of a man finally coming to terms with his lot? A man at last accepting that most unacceptable of truths – that life *is* unjust? Or was there a darker, more dangerous emotion starting to emerge from this hitherto undemonstrative man. Was this an anger, an envy, even a dim forgotten desire for revenge ...? (*She pauses, dramatically.*)

As Jill has spoken the lights have slowly widened, as before.

Cut. (*She rises and talks to the crew.*) That OK?

A shouted reply.

Yes, thank you very much. I meant technically OK, Dan – I can do without the editorial, thank you. Can we set up in the study now, please? We'll just do Vic's interview, then that's it for today, all right? (*waving them round*) Go through the front. Through the front door, it'll be easier. I'll see you there.

Jill gathers up her folder from the table. She flicks through it to find her questions for Vic. Kenny wanders out with a drink in his hand.

law-abiding always obeying the law **undemanding** modest **to take s.th. in** to absorb, to notice **vista** view **opulence** great wealth **to come to terms (with)** to accept **to emerge** to rise **hitherto** (*adv, fml*) until now **undemonstrative** not showing one's feelings **editorial** comment, e.g. an article in a newspaper

KENNY (*watching her*) Are you thinking of doing your interview with Vic fairly soon?

JILL Yes. They're just setting it up ...

KENNY You'd better get a move on. The rate he's pouring it down himself, he won't be able to string two words together ...

JILL God, I asked him to go easy –

KENNY Oh, yes? I'll tell him you're nearly ready. In the study?

JILL I'll be right there. He is forty-seven, isn't he?

KENNY Forty-seven, yes. Forty-eight next May.

JILL (*scribbling this on to her notes*) Does he mind it being mentioned?

KENNY He never has done.

JILL If I get Vic done now, then tomorrow morning I can spend with Mr Beechey and that leaves me the rest of the day clear – till our flight, to do general shots of the island ... Should be all right. Always providing I can get Mr Beechey to say anything remotely interesting ...

KENNY He tries his best, I think.

JILL It was a complete waste of time just now with the three of us. It was all Vic talking. Beechey never said a word –

KENNY Well, Vic's an expert, isn't he? I mean, he's done hundreds of these things. How many's Douglas done?

JILL I gave him his chance. Douglas, what do *you* think? Douglas, what do *you* say to that? You heard me. Nothing. Not a usable syllable. (*excitedly*) I tell you, Kenny, somehow or other – if I'm going to make any sort of programme – I have got to find a way to prise that man open. Get to the heart of him. I know, you see, I know that under all that suburban – blandness – that dreary flock-wallpaper personality of his – there is a real person there. There is pain – there is disappointment – there is a burning resentment – hopefully even hatred, who knows.

KENNY Really? Are you sure?

JILL There has to be. Please God there is.

KENNY He seems pretty well-balanced to me.

to go easy (on) to be careful (with) **to prise s.th. open** to open s.th. by force **suburban** (*derog*) boring, uninspired, like the endless rows of houses in the suburbs of London **blandness** lack of any strong characteristics, emotions, etc. **dreary** (*infml*) uninteresting **flock-wallpaper** a kind of wallpaper typical of "suburban" houses, with thin decorative material glued onto the surface and printed over, to produce a faintly three-dimensional effect **resentment** anger at having been insulted **please God** (*fml*) let's hope

JILL There has to be. Or the man wouldn't be human.

Douglas comes out of the house. He has again removed his jacket.

(*switching her tone with accustomed ease*) Mr Beechey, I was just saying – I want to save you till tomorrow morning. All right? When you're fresh.

DOUGLAS Just to suit you, Jill. I'll fit in with you. I must say though, after that lunch – not to mention that wine – I think you might be wiser to let me sleep it off. What a host, eh? What a host Vic is. It seems like every day is Christmas Day in this house.

JILL Don't you drink, normally?

DOUGLAS Oh, Nerys and I are not averse to the odd glass of mother's ruin. But not quite in this quantity. (*He laughs.*)

KENNY I'll – er ... see if Vic's ready.

JILL Thanks.

Kenny goes back into the house.

DOUGLAS So we'll all be flying home tomorrow, eh?

JILL That's right.

DOUGLAS Maybe we'll be on the same flight.

JILL No. I think we're going a little later than you. We've got the odd bit of filming to do tomorrow afternoon.

DOUGLAS All go, eh?

JILL Well ...(*She appears to be considering saying something.*)

DOUGLAS Then what do you do?

JILL Er – then we have a look at what we've got – And edit. And then we cut it together using any additional studio sequences we decide to include – using actors – what we call reconstructed action ...

DOUGLAS Actors playing us?

JILL Probably ...

DOUGLAS Fascinating. Make sure you get a good-looking one for me, won't you? (*He laughs.*)

JILL (*smiling wearily*) And then I link the whole thing together, live, on the day ...

DOUGLAS Live. Goodness.

to switch to change quickly **averse to** opposed to **mother's ruin** "rhyming slang" for gin **sequence** a group of scenes or events **to link** to connect *here:* (*TV*) by a live commentary

JILL Well, recorded live. In front of a studio audience, anyway.

DOUGLAS What about that, then? All that work just for one programme. People just don't realize, do they?

A slight pause. When Jill speaks, it is in her most simple, honest tone. As of one who really is asking for his help.

JILL Douglas ...?

DOUGLAS Yes?

JILL May I ask you something? Do you think – do you feel that I've been asking you the right questions?

DOUGLAS How do you mean?

JILL Well, let me try and explain. Usually, someone like me, a professional interviewer – well, we try as best we can to get at what we hope is the truth, the core of the person we're interviewing. We ask them what we hope are the right questions and then, hopefully, they respond. Which in turn leads us to ask further questions and slowly we arrive at what we, the interviewer, wants to hear; and, more important, hopefully what you, the interviewee, wants to say. Now, I don't feel in our case that I've really got at the truth of you. Do you see? I haven't – I don't feel I've allowed you, yet, to say what you really, truthfully want to say. Now that is not a fault in you, Douglas. That, I'm ashamed to admit, is a fault in me, the interviewer. And I know, I should be able to cope with that. That's my job. That's what I was trained to do. But in our case, yours and mine, it's just not working. I admit it. And it's very unprofessional of me – but I'm actually appealing to you directly for help.

DOUGLAS (*perturbed*) I see. I see. I thought we'd been getting on rather well.

JILL Douglas, be honest. I have done nothing more than scratch the surface of you. Be honest. Have I?

DOUGLAS Er ...

JILL Some people (*she clicks her fingers*) – you know. No problem. It's all there for the picking – open-cast mining. But I have to say it, in your case, you're a very, very, deep shaft indeed, Douglas. Too deep for me.

core the centre, the innermost part **interviewee** the person being interviewed **perturbed** (*fml*) worried **for the picking** to be picked up without an effort, easy to get **open-cast** (*techn, mining*) open-hole, without digging passages below ground **shaft** (*techn, mining*) a long narrow passage or hole, sloping or vertical

DOUGLAS Well, how extraordinary. I've never thought of myself as that ...You may be right. Maybe you just haven't been asking the correct questions.

JILL Take you and Nerys, for instance.

DOUGLAS Yes?

JILL I mean, you've never really talked about your relationship with her. Are you happy together, for instance?

DOUGLAS Yes.

JILL Truly happy?

DOUGLAS Yes.

JILL No problems?

DOUGLAS No. Not really. I can't think of any, offhand.

JILL Despite the fact that she can't face leaving the house?

DOUGLAS Well, that's true, yes. But we've both learnt to live with that, you see ...

JILL Doesn't it upset her?

DOUGLAS No. She doesn't seem to mind. She doesn't want to go anywhere.

JILL Doesn't she get lonely?

DOUGLAS No. She's never said so.

JILL What, all alone in that little house? Every day, while you're out at work?

DOUGLAS She isn't all alone. People come to visit her.

JILL Who do?

DOUGLAS Friends, relations ...

JILL She has friends?

DOUGLAS Dozens of them. They're always dropping in to see her. There are two of them staying there now.

JILL Women?

DOUGLAS Yes, of course, women ... And possibly her uncle Reg, if he can take the day off from the pet shop.

JILL But surely, Douglas ... Douglas, there must be more in life for you both than just sitting together day after day in that damp little house ...?

DOUGLAS No, it's not damp. That's one of the good things about it ...

JILL But coming here – seeing all this – the pool, the villa, the sunshine ...Wouldn't you like this for Nerys, at least? Even if not for yourself? Doesn't she deserve it after what she went through? Wouldn't you both adore to have all this, in your heart of hearts?

to adore (to do) (*infml*) to love, to like (to do) very much

DOUGLAS Frankly, no, I'm sorry, we wouldn't. Neither of us swims, Nerys is allergic to sunlight and, personally, I can't get on with Spanish food, not at all.

JILL (*growing desperate*) Well, somewhere else. Italy?

DOUGLAS No.

JILL Greece? Sweden?

DOUGLAS No, no. Not attracted, sorry. Despite their standard of living, they always look a rather glum sort of people, don't you think? They certainly do on television.

JILL Well, you can't always go by everything – (*She checks herself.*) Possibly.

DOUGLAS You know, I have to say this, you're making me feel rather guilty, Jill. I'm sorry if I'm being a disappointment. I'd have thought, though, that with all that misery you seem to meet up with in your job every day, a happy, contented couple might make a nice change for once. Wouldn't you have thought?

JILL (*in exasperation*) Sorry, Douglas, no. They wouldn't. Not at all. Happy, contented couples – happy, contented, middle-aged couples especially – do not make exciting films, they do not make watchable plays or readable books. Nobody wants to hear about them. Nobody's interested in them. Nobody even wants to look at paintings of them. And they certainly don't want to sit down and watch them on television. Happy, contented people are box-office death, Douglas. Because they generally come over as excruciatingly boring. They come over as smug and self-satisfied and superior and they drive the rest of us up the bloody wall and we really don't want to know about them. Not at all. All right?

A pause. Douglas considers this calmly, seemingly unoffended.

DOUGLAS (*quietly*) How sad. That's all I can say. How very sad.

JILL (*realizing that she has been very rude, even by her standards*) I'm sorry.

DOUGLAS No …

glum depressed, sad **to check oneself** to control, stop oneself **exasperation** anger and frustration **box-office** (*theatre*) the place where one buys the tickets **excruciatingly** (*adv*) very badly, painfully **smug** (*derog*) narrow-minded **superior** (*here: derog*) believing oneself to be superior to others **to drive s.b. up the wall** (*infml*) to make s.b. very angry and frustrated **rude** opposite of polite

JILL If you and Nerys really are that rare and precious thing, a blissfully happy married couple, who am I to come between you …? (*gathering up her things*) Well, I must see how my crew are getting on …

DOUGLAS Good luck.

Jill goes to leave but turns back again, just before she does so.

JILL (*incredulously*) No, I'm sorry, I can't believe it. You are both *completely* happy?

DOUGLAS (*worriedly*) Yes, I think we are. I was trying to think …

JILL Excuse me, but – sexually, as well?

DOUGLAS (*blankly*) Sexually?

JILL Sexually, you know. Sex? Long winter evenings? And so on?

DOUGLAS Well, no, we don't – No.

JILL You don't?

DOUGLAS No.

JILL You mean you don't sleep together?

DOUGLAS Yes, we sleep together, we just don't – No.

JILL Ever?

DOUGLAS No. Not for some little while.

JILL What do you mean by some little while?

DOUGLAS Er – probably about fifteen years, probably.

JILL (*stunned*) Fifteen years.

DOUGLAS Yes, I should think – I should think about that, yes.

JILL (*appalled*) My God, how have you both managed …?

DOUGLAS Oh, I don't think it's ever been a problem –

JILL Fifteen years? I don't believe it. *Fifteen years?* (*Pause.*) You're joking. Fifteen *years?* Did you never try to talk to anyone about it?

DOUGLAS No, we never felt the need. Anyway, I don't think anyone would be very interested. We – you know – we tried it for a couple of years when we first got married and – neither of us – found much to it, really – rather overrated, really – so we gave it up …

JILL Sorry. I have to sit down. (*She does so.*)

DOUGLAS You all right?

blissfully happy completely happy **incredulously** (*adv*) not believing **blankly** (*adv*) not understanding **stunned** extremely surprised **appalled** shocked **over-rated** not deserving its reputation

JILL (*laughing weakly*) Yes. I couldn't include this in a programme, they wouldn't believe it ...

DOUGLAS Oh, I don't know. It's not that uncommon, you know. Nerys's Uncle Reg told me he'd never tried it at all and he's never missed it ...

JILL Maybe it's genetic. (*Slight pause.*) *Fifteen years?* And you have never had it? Do you realize, Douglas, there are some of us, many of us, who spend all our waking hours thinking about having it and at night, if we're not having it, we dream about having it? We spend most of our lives trying to work out how we can get someone to have it with us and then, once we've had it, how we can get rid of the person we're having it with, so we can have it with somebody else? And you've never even bothered to have it ... I don't believe it. And Nerys feels the same? She doesn't miss it either?

DOUGLAS She's never said she has.

JILL What about children? Did she never want children?

DOUGLAS (*quickly*) No. Never. She –

JILL What?

DOUGLAS She never did. (*Pause.*) I think that maybe as a result of – her accident ... she felt unable to cope with the responsibility of children.

JILL And you?

DOUGLAS Oh, I quite understood why. I appreciated her decision.

JILL But would you have liked children, if she'd been willing?

DOUGLAS Possibly.

JILL You'd have liked them? In other circumstances?

DOUGLAS (*cautiously*) Yes ...

JILL If, for instance, she hadn't been injured, you'd both probably have had them?

DOUGLAS (*uncomfortably*) Er – who can say? Possibly.

JILL (*seeing some light at last*) Yes. Right. (*moving into the house once more, briskly*) We might talk further about children tomorrow, Douglas. In our interview. All right?

DOUGLAS (*unhappily*) Yes. Yes, if you like.

genetic passed on from parents to children in the genes **cautiously** (*adv*) watchfully **briskly** (*adv*) full of energy

Jill goes into the house. She seems rather triumphant. Douglas wanders out towards the pool. He is thoughtful. It is mid-afternoon, and very hot. Ruy comes through the garden gate with a block of rough stone, one of several such journeys he will make during the next.

Hallo.

Ruy, as always, doesn't even acknowledge Douglas's presence.

Dried off, I hope? (*He laughs.*)

A bird sings. A plane drones overhead. Douglas looks up again. Vic comes out on to the terrace, followed by Kenny. Vic has apparently had a bit to drink.

KENNY She says they're nearly ready.

VIC Well, they know where I am if they want me, don't they? It's too hot to sit in there.

He sits in the shade. Kenny does likewise.

(*calling to Douglas*) Get sunstroke if you stand around out there too long, mate.

DOUGLAS (*turning*) Pardon?

VIC I said, be careful in the sun. If you're not used to it.

DOUGLAS Oh, yes. Thank you. (*returns to the terrace and sits with them*) I thought you'd be doing your interview.

KENNY They're not quite ready.

DOUGLAS Oh.

Pause.

Do you think ours went all right? Our interview?

VIC (*without enthusiasm*) It was all right.

DOUGLAS You were wonderful. Never stuck for an answer.

VIC Well ...

KENNY He's done it before. Once or twice.

DOUGLAS Yes, I'm afraid that showed, so far as I was concerned. I'm afraid she floored me once or twice. I was completely

to drone (*adv*) to make a low monotonous sound, *G.* summen **to floor s.b.** (*infml*) to knock s.b. down

speechless. She said she'd be able to cut them out, though. My hesitations. Ah.

Marta has come from the house with a freshly opened bottle of wine and some glasses on a tray. She places them beside Vic. During the next, Ruy returns empty-handed from the swimming pool and goes out through the gate.

MARTA Mr Vic …

VIC Thank you, Marta. Is my wife coming out here, then?

MARTA Mrs Parks is doing washing up, Mr Vic.

VIC Why is she doing the washing up?

MARTA I don't know, Mr Vic …

VIC You should be doing the bloody washing up, not her. That's what you're paid for.

MARTA I don't know, Mr Vic …

VIC You do the washing up, all right? Tell her to come out here.

MARTA (*going back inside*) Yes, Mr Vic …

Vic pours himself a glass of wine.

VIC I don't know … (*holding up the bottle rather belatedly*) Anybody?

DOUGLAS No, thank you.

KENNY (*gently*) Go steady, Vic.

VIC (*mimicking*) Go steady. You sound like my auntie, you great fruit … (*He drinks.*) No, I'll tell you something about interviews and being interviewed. The first thing you've got to remember is that, generally speaking, if you are the one being interviewed and feeling nervous, then the person interviewing you – nine times out of ten – he's even more nervous than you are. Because if it all goes wrong, if you cock the whole thing up, all you stand to do is make a fool of yourself – whereas for him – well, it's his job on the line, isn't it? Know what I mean?

Ruy returns through the gate with another piece of stone. He exits round the swimming pool.

belatedly (*adv*) too late **go steady** be more careful **fruit** 1. (*BrE, old-fash, sl*) (old) friend 2. (*AmE, derog*) male homosexual **to cock s.th. up** (*sl*) to spoil, make a bad job of s.th. **to stand to do** to have a chance of getting/losing **on the line** *here:* in danger

DOUGLAS Yes, I see. That hadn't occurred to me, I must say.

KENNY (*who has been watching Ruy*) What's he doing there?

VIC Ruy? He's building a bench – a little stone seat, the other end of the swimming pool …

DOUGLAS Clever.

VIC Well, he's really a stone mason. But he's had a spot of bother with the local law … No, the other thing you've got to remember about an interview is that, normally, whoever's interviewing you will know less about what you're talking about than you do. Because nine times out of ten, he'll be talking to you about you – which makes you the resident expert, doesn't it? As far as you're concerned, it's a home game. He'll be nervous just coming down the tunnel, even before he's started. You see, there's an art to being interviewed. First, you've got to be able to use an interview to your own advantage. I mean, after all, what is an interview? This guy is more often than not trying to get you to say one thing – usually incriminating. And you, on the other hand, are wanting to say something of your own, entirely different to what he wants you to say. So it's a battle to the death, isn't it? If you're being interviewed, you have to turn it around, see? You say things like – that's a very good question, John, and I'd like to answer it if I may – with a question of my own. That always throws them, because they can't bear getting questions back at them. Because they're not usually geared for answers. Only for questions. Because they're interviewers, see, and not meant to have opinions. So they can't answer, anyway. But when they don't, that makes them look furtive. And when he does get a question in, if you don't like the one he's asked you, then give him an answer to another one … And when he interrupts you – which he will do, once he realizes that you're giving him the wrong answer, you say to him, I really must be allowed to answer this question in my own way, John, please. And look a bit hurt whilst you're saying it. 'Cause that'll make him look a pushy bastard, too. And another tip, if you're giving an answer and you do happen to know the answer and don't mind giving it

a spot of (*infml*) a little **bother** difficulty, trouble **home game** a match to be played on one's home-ground, at home **tunnel** *here:* the underground passage from which professional football-players enter the field **incriminating** (*law*) making one appear guilty **to throw s.b.** (*infml*) to confuse s.b. **to be geared for** (*infml*) to be prepared for **furtive** not honest, not saying one's mind **pushy** (*derog*) agressive, determined

to him, talk as fast as you can while still making sense, but don't whatever you do leave pauses. Because they're looking for pauses, see, to edit you about and change your meaning. That's when they put in those nodding bits, you've seen them, when the bloke's nodding his head for dear life about bugger all and sitting in a different room. But if you don't pause, they can't get in to edit, can they? And if they can't edit you, they've either got to leave the interview out altogether, which means they haven't got a programme, which is generally disaster time, or they have to put in what you said in its entirety and not some version of what some monkey would have liked you to have said if he'd got the chance to edit you. And if you're in full flow and you do run out and you do have to stop, stop suddenly. Just like that. (*Quick pause.*) OK? Because that throws him as well. Because nine out of ten, if it's a long answer you've been giving him, he won't be listening, anyway. He'll either be looking at his notes or at the floor manager, or wondering how long's this bleeder going on for? And if none of that works and you're really up against it, have a choking fit, throw yourself on the floor, knock the mic over and call for water. That usually does the trick.

A pause. Douglas digests this.

DOUGLAS There's a lot more to it than you imagine, isn't there?

KENNY True, very true.

Ruy crosses back to the garden gate, empty-handed again. They watch him. Vic pours himself another glass of wine. Sharon comes out of the house and walks through the men. She is still in her uniform and is evidently very hot. Her face is lobster-coloured and she is moving slowly and heavily. She ignores them as she passes through and heads towards the swimming pool. But there is something self-conscious in her walk that tells us she is aware of their eyes on her. She stoops to pick up one of the children's toys.

DOUGLAS (*as she does this*) Yes, but I think for the layman, such as myself, it's probably better just to answer the –

to edit (*techn*) to choose, i.e. cut out or include material for a film **bloke** (*infml*) man **bugger all** (*taboo sl*) nothing **disaster** catastrophe **bleeder** (*sl*) unpleasant person **choking fit** *G.* Erstickungsanfall **to digest** *here:* to think about and understand **lobster** *G.* Hummer **to stoop** to bend down

VIC (*watching Sharon*) Dear, oh dear, oh dear …

DOUGLAS Pardon?

VIC Just look at the ass on that girl …

KENNY (*less enthusiastically*) Yes.

VIC Look at it. Acres of it, isn't there?

Sharon goes off round the side of the swimming pool.

(*watching her go*) Dear, oh dear … (*to Douglas, who has been rather embarrassed*) Sorry, Doug, you were saying … Sorry, I interrupted you.

DOUGLAS (*who has forgotten what he was saying*) No, I was – no, I was just saying, put like you were putting it, it all seems a bit like a game, doesn't it?

VIC What?

DOUGLAS Interviews. On television.

VIC Well, they are. Most of them. That shock you, does it?

DOUGLAS No. Only occasionally, you know, people might genuinely be trying to say something, mightn't they? That they felt deeply about?

Kenny laughs drily. Ruy returns with another block of stone.

I wouldn't like to think it was all just nothing more than a game.

VIC (*pouring himself another glass of wine*) We all play games, don't we? One way or the other? We all do it.

DOUGLAS Do you think so?

VIC Like – right now – I'm wondering what yours might be …

DOUGLAS (*startled*) What?

VIC No, seriously. I'm very, very curious. What are you after, sunshine? Smiling away there. What are you after?

KENNY Vic …

VIC Well, don't tell me he came out here just to tell me what a nice man I am. What a lovely place I've got. Don't tell me he came all this way for that, because, frankly I don't believe him.

KENNY He came to do the programme, Vic …

VIC Don't kid me. The programme? You mean to tell me he did all this for a programme? Just so he could see himself on the telly? I don't believe it …

ass (*AmE taboo sl*) arse **acre** 1 acre = 4050 m^2 **startled** surprised

DOUGLAS I'm sorry, but I did ...

VIC Well, I'm sorry, but I don't believe you.

DOUGLAS I did. (*Slight pause.*) Well, and to – (*He checks himself.*)

VIC What? And to what?

DOUGLAS And to – see you.

VIC To see me?

DOUGLAS Yes.

VIC I shouldn't have thought you'd have wanted to see me again, would you?

DOUGLAS Well, when Jill first wrote to us, I must say I didn't, no. But in the end – after Nerys and I had both talked about it – we decided I had to, really.

VIC Why?

DOUGLAS You – you're – This might sound peculiar, but ... Because you're still there. In our dreams, you see. After seventeen years. We still both dream about you. We wake up occasionally. In the night. Nerys has this terrible fear – it's quite ridiculous, I've told her – that one night you're going to break in downstairs and come up to get her. I've said to her, it's ridiculous – I mean, there you are on the telly twice a week or something, helping the kids or telling the old folk to mind how they go – I said, he's not going to want to break in here, Nerys – Not after seventeen years, is he? Still. You can't always control your imagination, can you? No matter how hard you try. So, don't take this wrong, but I was hoping this – meeting – might help to exorcize you. If you follow me. I told you it would sound peculiar.

A silence. Kenny looks at Vic a little apprehensively. Suddenly Vic laughs. He laughs loud and long. The wine helps. Ruy returns during this and goes out through the garden gate.

VIC Well, I ... (*He wipes his eyes.*) Well, I've been called a ... I've been called a lot of things ... (*controlling himself a little*) Look. Listen, Doug. I promise. I promise – you tell Nerys – tell her I'll never break in through her front window, all right? Tell her she's perfectly safe. I mean, I've been called a lot of things. (*to Kenny*) That's wonderful. Isn't that wonderful?

to exorcize s.b./s.th. to drive out (a ghost, demon) **apprehensively** (*adv*) worriedly

Sharon returns from the swimming pool. Walking slowly, as before, she carries an armful of the children's toys.

Hey, Sharon ...

SHARON (*stopping*) Yes, Mr Parks?

VIC Where're Timmy and Cindy?

SHARON They're having their tea in the kitchen with Marta, Mr Parks.

VIC Sit down, then.

SHARON I've got to go and –

VIC Sit down.

SHARON Yes, Mr Parks.

Sharon sits, still holding on to the toys. She is obviously hotter than ever and slightly breathless.

VIC Get your breath back.

SHARON Thank you ...

VIC Look at her. Puffing like a grampus, aren't you?

SHARON Yes, Mr Parks.

VIC Sweat running off you. (*to the others*) Look at her. Have you ever seen anyone sweating like that? It's dripping off her. I bet it's running off you underneath there, isn't it, eh? Eh?

Sharon doesn't reply.

Running down your arms? Trickling down your legs? If there's one thing I hate, it's to see a woman sweating like that. It's bad enough on a man, it's obscene on a woman, don't you agree?

Sharon sits unhappily. Ruy crosses with another block of stone.

I'll tell you something, Sharon. Do you know why you're sitting there, sweating like that? Do you know the reason why you're sat there like a great bowl of pork dripping? Do you want to know the reason? Because you are overweight, girl. You are fat. Let's face it, Sharon, you are a fat girl, aren't you? A big, fat girl.

DOUGLAS Oh, I don't think that's fair, she's just ...

VIC Here, let her tell you something, just a second. Sharon ...

SHARON Yes, Mr Parks ...

to puff like a grampus *here G.* wie ein Walross schnauben **to be sat** to be made to sit, to be placed **dripping** the fat dripping from a piece of meat being cooked

VIC Shall we tell them why you're so fat? Shall we? Shall we tell them your secret? It's because you are greedy, isn't it, Sharon? You eat too much. You are a guts. Aren't you? You're a glutton. Eh?

SHARON Yes, Mr Parks.

VIC Tell them what you ate on your last birthday, Sharon. Tell them. This girl, she told me that last year on her birthday, she sat on her own, in her flat in wherever it was – Macclesfield –

SHARON Huddersfield ...

VIC Huddersfield. She sat there all on her own, singing happy birthday to me and she ate ... What did you eat, Sharon? Tell them what you ate, go on.

SHARON (*muttering*) Twelve rum babas.

VIC Come on, say it louder ...

SHARON (*loudly*) Twelve rum babas, Mr Parks.

VIC Twelve rum babas. Can you imagine that? Turns you over, doesn't it? Still, we're working on you, aren't we, Sharon? We're slowly melting you down, aren't we?

SHARON Yes, Mr Parks ...

VIC Getting her fit. Giving her some exercise. Working it off her. What were you learning this morning then? What was I teaching you this morning, Sharon?

SHARON Scuba diving, Mr Parks.

VIC Scuba diving. She enjoyed that – didn't you?

SHARON Yes.

VIC You should have seen her in her big black rubber suit flailing about in the water there, first thing. Like a big shiny, beached, humpbacked whale, weren't you ...

Sharon suddenly starts to cry very quietly.

DOUGLAS Look, I'm sorry, this is very, very cruel and unnecessary and I really don't think you should go on tormenting this girl simply because –

VIC You mind your own business –

greedy wanting to eat too much **guts** (*sg*) a person who eats too much, (abbreviated from greedy-guts) **glutton** (*derog*) a person who eats too much **rum baba** a rich kind of cake usually soaked in rum **to turn s.b. over** (*sl*) to make s.b. sick **scuba diving** swimming under water using a container of compressed air with a rubber pipe for breathing **beached** stuck on land **humpbacked** hunch-backed, with a large lump rising from a person's back **to torment s.b.** to annoy s.b., to cause pain to s.b.

DOUGLAS (*undaunted*) – simply because she's a shade overweight and obviously very self-conscious about it, anyway. It is cruel and it is hurtful and it is –

VIC (*suddenly yelling at him*) I said, mind your own bloody business!

A silence. Sharon gets up and runs into the house. She passes Trudy who is coming out. Trudy looks at the men and appears to sum up the scene. Ruy crosses again, empty-handed.

(*to Douglas, softly*) I hope I don't have to remind you again that you are a guest in this house. And the way I choose to treat my staff is entirely my concern. OK?

Douglas is silent. Kenny clears his throat.

KENNY They should be about set up for that interview, I should think …

TRUDY They were nearly ready, yes.

VIC I've been waiting here. Patiently. Plenty of things I could have been getting on with, too.

TRUDY (*brightly*) I wondered if you wanted to take up my offer and stroll down to the beach, Douglas? While they're doing their interview?

DOUGLAS Oh, lovely, yes. Thank you very much.

VIC (*sourly*) Yes, you take him down the beach, good idea.

TRUDY (*faintly sarcastic*) Oh, dear. You haven't been disagreeing with my husband, have you? I hope not.

DOUGLAS No, I –

TRUDY You mustn't do that, you know. He only likes people who agree with him all the time. It's one of his little whims.

VIC What are you talking about?

TRUDY It comes of being surrounded by people who nod at him all day at work. He prefers us all to nod at home, too …

VIC (*innocently*) What did I do, eh? What am I meant to have done, now?

KENNY (*laughing*) Can't imagine.

TRUDY He surrounds himself with these little nodding animals. It's like the back shelf of a car in our house. We all do it.

undaunted not discouraged in the least **to stroll** to go for a leisurely walk **whim** sudden mood

VIC Bloody rubbish.

TRUDY Yes, quite right, dear. Nod, nod.

VIC What a load of rubbish. (*to Kenny*) Isn't it? A load of rubbish?

KENNY (*nodding*) Oh, yes.

TRUDY (*to Douglas*) It's about a mile's walk down there. Do you mind?

DOUGLAS No, I'd like a walk.

VIC Take the jeep.

TRUDY No, we want a walk.

VIC Be quicker in the jeep …

TRUDY No, we want to walk. It's healthier …

VIC Healthier? What are you talking about, healthier?

TRUDY Healthier. Walking.

VIC All right then, walk if you want to walk. I think everyone around here is just trying to wind me up, for some reason …

Ruy has entered with another block of stone.

(*yelling jovially*) That's it, Ruy, lad. Get stuck in there, boy.

RUY (*beaming, despite the exertion*) Yes Mr Vic. You bet.

Ruy goes out.

TRUDY What's he building now? Not another garden seat?

VIC Why not?

TRUDY Because he keeps building them and then you tell him to pull them down again.

VIC Because they were in the wrong place, that's why.

TRUDY Well, I hope this one's in the right place.

VIC I'll tell you that when he's built it.

Jill comes out from the house.

JILL Vic, Kenny – I'm most dreadfully sorry to have kept you waiting. Believe it or not, we are now finally ready to go when you are.

VIC Hooray –

JILL First, we had glare from the window, so we moved round and then we couldn't get back far enough for the two shot …

VIC (*rising, impatiently*) Come on. Let's get it over with …

rubbish *here:* nonsense **to wind s.b. up** (*infml, BrE*) to make fun of **exertion** hard work, effort **glare** (*techn*) too much light

Vic goes inside, taking his glass with him. He passes Marta, who comes out to clear the tray and remaining glasses.

JILL Kenny, you'll want to sit in of course …

KENNY Well, I'd better. Just in case he says something your lawyers will regret later –

JILL (*laughing*) Oh, hardly. Surely not.

KENNY He's been known to. On occasions …

Kenny goes into the house. Jill is about to follow but lingers to watch Trudy and Douglas. Trudy has moved off the patio to look at what Ruy is building. Douglas has moved to join her. Marta, in due course, follows Kenny into the house.

TRUDY (*turning to Douglas, smiling*) Well, shall we go?

DOUGLAS (*smiling back*) Ready when you are.

Trudy and Douglas go out through the gate. Jill watches them go. The lights close down on to her, like a smooth, zooming close up.

JILL (*solemnly, to camera*) After seventeen long years, the strands were finally being drawn together – individual threads in a tapestry shaped over the years by the hands of countless separate participants – none of whom perhaps, individually, was consciously aware of the final picture which was slowly and inevitably being woven around them. And that picture? No less a portrait than the face of human tragedy … (*she pauses.*) (*calling*) I may need to do that bit again later, George … (*yelling back to them as she goes inside*) Sorry. Cut!

The lights change abruptly on her shout. It is suddenly a moonlit evening. Patches of shadow. Cicadas chirping. Very romantic. Perhaps marred slightly by some very syrupy country and western music emanating distantly from the hi-fi somewhere in the house. Pause.

tapestry wall-covering made of cloth, like a carpet **patch** small different-coloured segment of a surface **to emanate from** to come from

In a moment, Trudy and Douglas come through the gate. They have evidently just returned from their walk.

DOUGLAS I'm afraid we've taken rather longer than we should have done.

TRUDY No, we've only been a couple of hours. It gets dark much quicker out here. You get used to it after a bit. (*Looking towards the house.*) It doesn't sound as if anyone's missed us particularly, does it?

DOUGLAS They can't still be filming, surely?

TRUDY (*looking back through the gate*) The crew must have gone back to the hotel. Their van's gone, anyway. And her hire car. She's gone too. Thank God.

DOUGLAS Ah, well. My turn tomorrow. In the hot seat.

TRUDY Are you looking forward to it?

DOUGLAS (*uncertain*) Well ...

TRUDY I wouldn't be, I must say.

DOUGLAS I think the problem is that – well, what Jill would really like is a bit of conflict. She was saying to me at lunch that a good programme has got to have a bit of conflict. It needs conflict, otherwise people tend to switch off, apparently. Mind you, I don't. There's nothing I like better than a programme with no conflict in it at all. Nerys is the same. But obviously we're in a minority there. Everyone else seems to prefer to see people beating each other's brains out. Extraordinary. So, to create a bit of conflict, I think Jill would really like me to say a lot of things I don't particularly care to say. That's the trouble.

TRUDY Like what?

Douglas makes to move on towards the house.

(*stopping him*) No, stay here a minute ... Like what? What does she want you to say?

DOUGLAS Oh ...

TRUDY No, you must tell me. I need to know. We must talk, you see. Mustn't we? It's been a lovely walk but we haven't really talked, have we? And we need to. We do, you know. And it has to be you and me. You can never talk to Vic, not about something he doesn't want to talk about, anyway. Nobody can. I mean,

to care (in negative sentences) to like

I'd have talked to your wife if she'd been here. But she isn't. And she obviously doesn't want to meet us or have anything to do with us, which is perfectly understandable. So it has to be us two, you see. Doesn't it? (*Pause.*) I mean, I need to know how you feel. How you really feel. You're very good at covering up, but ... (*Pause.*) Do you see why I need to know? You must see. I have to know if you've forgiven us, you understand?

DOUGLAS Us?

TRUDY Yes. I'm a part of Vic. I married him, knowing what he'd done to another human being. To another woman. And I had his children knowing that. I took on all of him. What do they say these days? (*smiling faintly*) A wife should be responsible for her husband's debts. (*Pause.*) So I need to know.

DOUGLAS I think, quite honestly, what's past is past, isn't it?

TRUDY You really don't bear any resentment for what he did? To you? To your wife? The woman you were in love with? Didn't it matter? It's like it never mattered to you at all.

DOUGLAS Oh, it mattered. Then. Of course it did. Only – Well, it wasn't as straightforward as that. It never is. Let me try and – explain, then. It's difficult. (*Pause.*) Working with me in this bank – I was twenty-four – twenty-five at the time – working with me, alongside me – was the most beautiful woman I have ever seen in my life, anywhere. Before or since. Her name was Nerys Mills and she was a stunner. And I was – besotted. That's the only word for it. Some days I couldn't look at her at all. My hands would shake and my voice used to crack and go falsetto when I spoke and I'd feel sick in my stomach, and one day I actually started crying without any warning at all. Right in the middle of serving a customer. In the end, I had to pretend I got hay fever. And that was very inconvenient, because then I had to remember to keep having it and take nose drops and things, otherwise people would begin to wonder what was really wrong with me. Anyway, needless to say – Nerys didn't take a blind bit of notice of me. No, that's not exactly true. She was generally

to cover up s.th. to hide s.th., keep it to oneself **to bear resentment** (*fml*) to continue to feel resentment **stunner** (*old-fash, infml*) a stunningly beautiful person **besotted** foolishly drunk, drunk with love **to crack** to break **to go falsetto** *here:* to change suddenly to a different level **falsetto** *G.* Fistelstimme **hay fever** an illness producing the symptoms of a cold, caused by pollen **inconvenient** annoying, making life difficult, taking up time **to take notice of s.b./s.th.** (in negative sentences) to listen to s.b./s.th. **blind** (*sl*) slightest

very nice and polite, but, so far as romance went, I think I was definitely at the bottom of the reserves as far as she was concerned. She was actually unofficially engaged to this other man – (*darkly*) I forget his name now. I never forget names but I've forgotten his.

TRUDY Did he work in the bank as well?

DOUGLAS No, no. He was a salesman. A double-glazing salesman, actually. There's an amusing story to that, I'll come back to that. Anyway, I sat there and – longed for her – day after day – month after month – fantasized about her a little – nothing unpleasant, you know ...

TRUDY No, no ...

DOUGLAS And some mornings she'd have a chat with me between customers. And then the sun would shine all day, you know ... (*He smiles.*)

TRUDY (*smiling*) Yes ...

DOUGLAS And other mornings, she'd come in like thunder – something obviously had gone wrong the night before with her and old double-glazing ... And then, of course, you never got a smile ...

TRUDY (*sadly*) Ah ...

DOUGLAS And as time went by, I marked her off in my own personal ledger in the desirable but unattainable column, along with the Silver Cloud and the offer to keep wicket for Kent – and I was just resigning myself to life without her and seriously considering whether the Royal Army Pay Corps might have a vacancy somewhere – when the bank raid occurred. And that did change everything. There's no doubt about it. I don't know why I did what I did. Your husband was right, it was madness. It just seemed the only thing to do at the time, that's all. There was this stranger in a balaclava threatening the woman that I cared more than my own life for ... I couldn't help myself, you see?

TRUDY (*engrossed*) No. I see. I see.

reserves players in a team who are only asked to play if the others cannot **to fantasize** to have day-dreams **ledger** book in which a firm's financial transactions are listed, *G.* Hauptbuch **unattainable** never to be had, out of reach **Silver Cloud** a Rolls-Royce car **to keep wicket for** to be a member of a county cricket-team **vacancy** job on offer (or room to let) **balaclava** warm wollen kind of cap leaving only the face free **to care for s.b.** to like, be fond of s.b. **engrossed** fascinated

DOUGLAS Afterwards, I went to see her a lot in hospital. Partly through guilt. Only partly. But, you see, if I hadn't run at Vic like that, she might never have – Not that she's ever blamed me. She's never once, ever – Never. Anyway, I went to see her, as soon as they'd let us in to visit. I imagined there'd be so many blokes round the bed she'd never even see me, anyway. And there were, to start with. I was just there waving my bunch of daffodils at her from the back of the crowd. And then slowly they all drifted away. Over the weeks. Stopped coming to see her.

TRUDY How rotten. Aren't people rotten, sometimes?

DOUGLAS Yes, I thought that at first. Then I realized later, of course. She'd been sending them all away. Subconsciously. A beautiful woman like she'd been, she couldn't bear to be seen like – that. She couldn't stand it. I mean, she wasn't vain. Not really. But if you're used all your life to people taking pleasure in looking at you, then it must be very hurtful when they suddenly start instinctively looking away from you. You couldn't blame people, altogether. She did look a terrible mess for a time.

TRUDY But you didn't? Look away from her?

DOUGLAS Well, I think I probably did, yes. As I say, it was only natural early on. But, you see, if I looked away from her, it didn't matter quite so much. Because she'd never valued my opinion of her anyway. So it never worried her. And there I was, with her all to myself. Visiting every day. Jollying her up. And over the weeks we got very friendly.

TRUDY And did she fall in love with you?

DOUGLAS I don't know.

TRUDY But did she never say to you … ?

DOUGLAS No. And I didn't ask her. It didn't matter. She liked me. And more important, she needed me. That's what mattered. And I loved her. (*He smiles.*) I was going to tell you, you know, when I'd left the bank, I applied for my present job with this double-glazing company. I thought it might – you know – increase my standing with her. Since she seemed to have a liking for double-glazing men. Ridiculous. We laughed about that later. I never

daffodil *G.* Narzisse **to drift away** to be driven away, e.g. by wind **rotten** (*infml*) mean, unpleasant **subconsiously** (*adv*) not consciously **to look a mess** (*infml*) to be untidy or dirty, or just unsatisfactory to look at **to jolly s.b. up** (*infml*) to encourage s.b., to make s.b. happy **standing** status, rank in other people's opinion

regretted it, though. They're a grand bunch. Anyway, she came out. And we married quietly. And we got a joint mortgage on number fifty-three and we've lived there ever since. With never a cross word, I'm happy to report. (*Pause.*) So what do I say? Yes, I do – I hate Vic because of what he did to the most beautiful woman in the world? Or, thank you very much, Vic, for being instrumental in arranging for me to marry the unattainable girl of my dreams? Difficult to know which to say, isn't it? (*Pause.*) All right. I know you might well say, what about her? What about poor old Nerys? Being forced to settle for minor league when she was naturally first division. Well, all I can say is, without prejudice, and I am not a swearing person, you appreciate – but that man she was engaged to originally – old double-glazing the first – he was a complete – pillock. He really was. He treated Nerys like – well, there were times when – not just me, you understand ... We all could have done – in that bank. Including Mr Marsh. This man – he treated her as only a handsome man can treat a beautiful woman. If you know what I mean.

TRUDY Yes. I do. I think I do.

They listen to the music for a moment.

DOUGLAS (*cheerfully*) Well, that's – that's my life. Sorry, if I bored you. (*Pause.*) This is very pleasant music, isn't it? Country and western? Am I right?

TRUDY (*weakly*) Yes. Vic likes it. We used to ... When we were ... (*Her voice tails away.*)

Douglas waits for her to finish the sentence. She doesn't. She is evidently in some distress. She rocks about. She looks at Douglas. Suddenly and unexpectedly, she kisses him on the mouth. Then pulls away and avoids his look. He, after taking a second to recover, avoids her in turn. They sit, pretending it hasn't happened.

mortgage a loan from a bank to buy a house, *G.* Hypothek **instrumental** being an instrument for a purpose **league** (*sport*) group of teams playing matches against each other **minor league** (*football*) the less competent teams **first division** (*football*) the best teams of the country, now called "Premier Division" **prejudice** an unfair opinion one holds against s.b. **to swear** to use swear-words, taboo words, etc. **pillock** (*sl*) useless, stupid person **to rock** to move gently back and forth or from side to side

DOUGLAS (*at length*) Yes, I'm very partial to country and western music. They always manage to come up with a good tune, don't they?

TRUDY (*in a little voice*) I'm sorry. (*then, pulling herself together*) There's nothing we can do for you, then? Vic and I? Nothing?

DOUGLAS Do?

TRUDY Well, to help in any way … Money or …

DOUGLAS (*rather embarrassed*) Oh, no.

TRUDY (*equally embarrassed*) Sorry. I didn't mean to –

DOUGLAS No, no …

TRUDY It's just so rare to meet someone who doesn't want something from us these days … I suppose that's called being successful. Or is it because it's us who are offering? Is that why you're saying you don't want anything?

DOUGLAS No, it's not that. I just don't think there is anything. Thank you very much. Well, I think I must away down the hill to my own hotel. They'll be serving dinner soon …

TRUDY You're welcome to stop and have supper with us if you –

DOUGLAS No, that's very kind of you, but you'll see quite enough of me again tomorrow.

TRUDY Well, wait there a second, I'll fetch the keys and run you back –

DOUGLAS No, please.

TRUDY It's no trouble –

DOUGLAS I'd rather walk, I really would. Really. I don't get the chance to walk around islands that much.

TRUDY (*reluctantly*) Well …

DOUGLAS Thank you for all your hospitality today. You've been very kind. You really have. (*He starts to move back towards the gate.*) Straight down the hill, I take it?

TRUDY Yes. Only when you get to the fork that leads to the sea – the one we took – go right instead of left.

DOUGLAS Simple enough. Well. See you tomorrow, Trudy.

TRUDY Goodnight, Douglas.

DOUGLAS (*turning in the gateway*) Er … (*smiling*) There's one thing I wouldn't have minded, I suppose. Not that you could have given it to me. But since you mentioned wanting things …

TRUDY What's that? Anything we –

to be partial to (*infml*) to like **reluctantly** (*adv*) unwillingly **fork (in a road)** place where a road splits into two branches

DOUGLAS No, I was just thinking. I was a hero, I suppose, for all of a year. People wrote to me. Sent for my photograph. Asked my advice. Listened to what I had to say. I think it would have been nice to have been a hero for a bit longer …

TRUDY You still are –

DOUGLAS … silly. I'd probably never have missed it, only …

TRUDY – to people like Nerys you are. And I bet there are others who still remember …

DOUGLAS No, I think I'm best remembered now as the idiot who tackled an armed robber and nearly got someone's head blown off in the process. I think you ended up with the hero, Trudy, not poor old Nerys. You stick with him. You stick with Vic. If you're looking for heroes. See you in the morning.

Douglas goes out through the gate. Trudy stares after him.

TRUDY (*faintly*) Yes …

She gets up to go into the house. Then decides that, if she's going to cry, she'd better cry out here. She sits down again in the shadows. She hugs herself and starts to weep quietly and privately.

In a little while, there is a faint slapping sound from the direction of the swimming pool. Trudy becomes aware of this and stops crying to listen. Sharon appears, walking along the side of the swimming pool towards the deep end. She has on her black wetsuit, rubber helmet and flippers. She carries a weighted diving belt. She is also crying. In fact, she is in a desperate, heartbroken state. She stops at the end of the swimming pool, a tragi-comic, fat, black, rubber-clad figure.

Trudy watches her, astonished. Sharon, unaware she is being watched, looks towards the house and starts to fasten the diving belt about her waist.

(*cautiously*) Sharon? Sharon … What are you doing there?

to tackle s.b./s.th. to try to deal with s.b./s.th. **to hug s.b.** to put one's arms around s.b. **privately** in private **flippers** rubber shoes with a large flat sole for fast under-water swimming **weighted** *here:* filled with heavy weights **-clad** (*lit*) dressed in, covered by

SHARON (*between sobs*) Mrs Parks …

TRUDY What are you doing, Sharon?

SHARON I'm going to kill myself Mrs Parks.

TRUDY (*moving to her, alarmed*) You are going to what?

SHARON I'm sorry, Mrs Parks. I love him so much, and he doesn't care about me at all.

TRUDY Sharon …

SHARON (*as in one breath*) He just says I'm fat and I've got to get thin and I've tried to get thin but I can't get thin whatever I do because when he says he doesn't love me I just keep eating because I'm so unhappy you see and then when I eat then I just get fatter you see and then he doesn't love me … and I love him so much, Mrs Parks, and I'm ever so sorry …

TRUDY Yes … I'm sorry, Sharon … I know how it is, believe me I do …

SHARON No, you don't – you can't …

TRUDY Yes, I do. I promise, Sharon, I do …

SHARON Nobody knows –

During the next, the music from the house stops as the record comes to an end.

TRUDY Sharon, it's a passing thing, I promise. It's something we all go through. Most of us, God help us. It'll pass …

SHARON No, it won't pass. I've loved Vic for years …

TRUDY Years? What do you mean, years? You've only been with us two months …

SHARON I seen him on the telly. I used to watch him on the telly and I used to write to him on *Ask Vic* and he used to write back to me, he did, I promise …

TRUDY Sharon, he gets thousands of letters a week. He doesn't even read them, let alone write back …

SHARON He did, he wrote to me and it was in his writing. And he used to tell us on the telly if we had problems how to deal with them and not to worry and then when I got this job working for him I just thought it was going to be so wonderful and he's just been horrible to me … I don't know what I've done … What have I done wrong, Mrs Parks?

During the next, Vic comes out of the house and listens, unnoticed.

to promise *here:* to declare honestly and sincerely

TRUDY (*fiercely*) The only thing you did wrong, Sharon ... the one and only thing you ever did wrong was to love him in the first place ... Because he is not a man to love, Sharon, I promise you. Not if you can possibly avoid it. I speak as one who has tried for eight years, Sharon, to keep loving him. While that bastard has abused me and ignored me and taken me for granted – while he has been screwing his way round Television Centre and half of ITV – I have looked after his kids and his house and his bloody, bad-tempered old mother in Beckenham ... And I have tried to keep loving him ... I swear to God I have tried. And if you are honestly clinging on to life in the hope of getting one tiny scrap of care or consideration back from that self-centred, selfish – scum bucket – then all I can say is, you'd better jump in there now, Sharon, and cut your losses.

Sharon, understandably, is a little bemused by this outburst. She stands indecisively. Vic steps out further on to the patio. Both women see him for the first time.

VIC Well, well. You know what they say. You never hear good about yourself, do you?

TRUDY Tell her, Vic. Talk to the girl, for God's sake.

VIC Tell her what?

TRUDY I just caught her trying to drown herself ...

VIC (*amused*) What?

TRUDY Vic, talk to her ...

VIC What do you want to drown yourself for, Sharon?

TRUDY What do you think ...?

VIC I have no idea. I have no idea why this great big girl should want to drown herself ...

Sharon sobs and finishes fastening her belt.

TRUDY Vic ...

VIC Why? Just tell me?

TRUDY Because of what you've said to her. Done to her.

VIC What?

to abuse s.b. *here:* to speak very unkindly to/about s.b. **to take s.b. for granted** to treat s.b. with selfish indifference **to screw s.b.** (*taboo sl*) to have sex with **ITV** "Independent Television" – the network of commercial TV companies **scum bucket** (*derog*) worthless person, *G.* Abschaum **to cut one's losses** to give up a bad or hopeless job or business **bemused** confused

TRUDY Whatever you said – whatever you did. I don't know. I don't want to know …

VIC I've never laid a finger on her, have I? Sharon, tell her, I've never laid a finger on you … Have I? Eh?

SHARON (*unhappily*) No, Mr Parks …

VIC There you are. No. She confirms that …

TRUDY (*shouting*) You know bloody well what you've done to her, Vic, now do something about it …

VIC Right, that's it, forget it. I am not being shouted at. Let her jump …

He turns to move into the house. Sharon prepares to jump into the pool.

TRUDY (*yelling*) Vic …

VIC (*furiously*) Let the stupid cow drown herself, what do I care? Go on. Jump, jump, jump then …

Sharon jumps into the pool. Weighted down by her diver's belt, she sinks rapidly under the dark water and vanishes in a trail of bubbles.

TRUDY (*screaming*) SHARON!

VIC (*surprised Sharon has done it*) Bloody hell!

Vic moves towards the pool.

TRUDY Vic, get her out. Dive in and get her out, for God's sake …

VIC I'm not diving in there. Not in these clothes.

TRUDY Vic, the girl is drowning.

VIC She's not drowning. She can stay under for hours. She's built like a bathyscope …

TRUDY Are you going in to get her, or not?

VIC You dive in.

TRUDY I can't get her out, she's far too big for me, she's enormous, Vic …

VIC We could sprinkle rum babas on the surface, that'll bring her up …

TRUDY You bastard … (*desperately*) Oh, dear God. (*running to the gate and yelling*) Douglas! Douglas! He's gone …

VIC (*peering into the pool, meanwhile*) Sharon! I can see you down there, Sharon.

bathyscope (*techn*) instrument or container for deep-sea diving **to sprinkle s.th.** to distribute s.th. thinly

TRUDY (*running to the house and calling*) Kenny! Kenny, come out here, please!

VIC Kenny went down to the shop – we were running out of vino …

TRUDY If she dies, Vic. If that girl dies …

VIC Nobody would miss her except the national union of bakers …

TRUDY (*running at him in fury*) You … God, I hate you! I really so hate you! (*She attacks him with both her fists.*)

VIC (*amused and fending her off easily*) Hey, hey, hey!

TRUDY (*beating at him*) I'd so love to … hurt you … like you … hurt … other people, sometimes …

She lands a blow that Vic doesn't care for. He takes her a little more seriously.

VIC Oi! Now, Trudy! That's enough. You've had your fun …

He starts to pinion her arms to protect himself. Trudy continues to fight and Vic is forced to turn her away from him and grab her neck in the crook of his arm in a traditional headhold whilst pinioning her arms with his other hand. Trudy is finally incapacitated. She remains there, exhausted and infuriated by her impotence against his superior strength.
Barely have they finished struggling when Douglas runs back into the garden through the gate. He is halfway to the house before he sees Vic and Trudy.

DOUGLAS (*as he enters*) What's the problem? I – (*He stops and stares at them in amazement.*)

TRUDY (*weakly, choking in Vic's grip*) Douglas … please!

VIC (*calmly*) Now, it's all right. Don't get excited and nobody'll get hurt, all right?

Douglas reacts like a charger on hearing the bugle call. He gives a sudden wild yell of fury and rushes at Vic head down.

to fend s.b./s.th. off to push or keep s.b./s.th. off **to pinion (the arms or legs)** (*fml*) to hold, to bind **to grab s.b./s.th.** to take hold of s.b./s.th. roughly **crook (of one's arm)** the angle formed by bending one's arm **incapacitated** made helpless **charger** (*lit*) soldier's horse **bugle call** trumpet-signal for the attack

DOUGLAS Aaaaarrrrgggghhhh!

VIC (*startled*) Jesus!

Vic pushes Trudy to one side in order to defend himself – not for the first time in his life – from Douglas's sudden wild onslaught. Douglas catches Vic in the midriff. Trudy screams. Vic grunts with pain, winded. Both men lose their balance. Vic topples into the pool. Douglas is left kneeling on the edge, slightly winded himself.

TRUDY Douglas? Are you all right?

DOUGLAS Yes, I … I'm … I'm sorry, I … Where's Vic?

TRUDY He's in the …

As she starts to speak, Vic's hand grips the edge of the pool. He hauls himself up. He looks very dangerous.

VIC (*breathless*) Right. There is about to be some serious damage done. I can tell you … (*pointing at Douglas and Trudy in turn*) To you. And to you. All right?

Douglas and Trudy draw back, nervously. Vic seems about to climb out of the pool.
Suddenly the waters part and a large black shape, barely recognizable as Sharon, breaks surface and seizes hold of Vic around the neck from behind.

As soon as I've … Uurrgghhh!

He is dragged under the water by Sharon's sheer weight.

DOUGLAS (*genuinely alarmed*) Oh, my goodness, what is it, a whale?

TRUDY No, it's Sharon …

onslaught furious attack **midriff** (*infml*) middle of the body, stomach **winded** short of breath **to topple** to move unsteadily and fall **to haul s.b./s.th.** to pull s.b./s.th. with an effort **recognizable** to be identified

There is a great deal of frenzied threshing about under the water. Rather like an old Johnny Weissmuller film. Trudy and Douglas watch, unable to do much else.

TRUDY (*during this, vainly*) Sharon ... Vic ...
DOUGLAS (*likewise*) Vic ... Sharon ...

The waters finally still. Sharon comes up for air and props herself against the side of the pool, breathlessly and strangely happy. Trudy and Douglas approach her cautiously..

TRUDY Sharon ...?
DOUGLAS Sharon ...?
TRUDY Are you all right?
SHARON (*gathering enough breath to speak*) Yes, thank you, Mrs Parks ...
DOUGLAS (*trying to calm her desperate breathing*) Easy. Easy now ...
TRUDY (*A sudden thought*) Sharon, where is Mr Parks?
SHARON (*apologetically*) I'm standing on him, Mrs Parks.

Trudy and Douglas react with alarm.

DOUGLAS Sharon, for goodness' sake ...
TRUDY (*with Douglas*) For God's sake, get off him ...

Together, they start to haul Sharon out of the water.

SHARON (*as they do so*) I'm very sorry, Mrs Parks ...
TRUDY All right, Sharon, all right. Out you come now.

They land her on the poolside like a large, beached mammal. Vic floats to the surface. Unconscious or worse. Sharon lies panting while Trudy and Douglas pull Vic from the water.

(*to Douglas*) Turn him over, we must get the water out of him ...
DOUGLAS Right.

frenzied very excited, mad **to thresh** to move arms and legs up and down in a kind of "beating" movement **Johnny Weissmuller** film star, famous as "Tarzan" **to still** (*lit*) to calm, to become calm **to prop o.s. against** to lean against **apologetically** (*adv*) being sorry **mammal** animal fed with milk by its mother as a baby

They turn Vic over.

SHARON (*as they do so*) Can I give him the kiss of life, Mrs Parks ...?

TRUDY No, you can't, Sharon. Stay there, please.

She and Douglas try to work on Vic rather ineffectually.

I don't know what you do. I think you have to pump his ribs somehow ...

DOUGLAS I'm afraid I don't really have much of an idea ... Me and water, you know ...

SHARON (*heaving herself up*) Here, let me ...

TRUDY No, Sharon, I'd rather you ...

SHARON It's all right, Mrs Parks, I've got my life-saver's medal.

TRUDY (*rather surprised*) You have?

SHARON In the Huddersfield baths. Here, let me ...

Sharon takes over from Trudy and Douglas. She sits astride Vic and pumps away vigorously. Trudy and Douglas watch her anxiously.

TRUDY Anything ...?

SHARON No, I don't think he's ... He's not responding.

TRUDY Oh, God.

SHARON Hang on.

She rolls Vic over and tries the kiss of life a couple of times. There is no response.

TRUDY (*anxiously*) No?

SHARON No. I'm sorry, Mrs Parks, I ... (*starting to cry as the realization finally hits her*) I'm sorry, I'm ever so sorry ... (*She kneels weeping again. A silence.*)

TRUDY I don't know what we're going to do. I don't know.

Silence.

What are we going to do?

DOUGLAS I suppose we'll have to report it. To the police, won't we?

kiss of life reviving a person by breathing into his/her mouth **ineffectually** (*adv*) being not very successful **to heave s.th.** to lift or pull s.th. heavy **to respond** show a healthy reaction to treatment **to report (a crime)** to inform the police

TRUDY If we report it, we'll have to tell them everything. We'll have to tell them it was Sharon. We can't have Sharon blamed for this ...

SHARON (*tearfully*) I didn't mean to, Mrs Parks ...

TRUDY (*comforting her*) It's all right, Sharon, it's all right. (*She considers.*) OK, I'll tell you what we're going to do. We're all going to have to tell the same story, all right? Douglas?

DOUGLAS Yes?

TRUDY Sharon? Are you listening to me?

SHARON Yes, Mrs Parks.

TRUDY We're going to have to say this. Vic was very drunk – that's true, anyway – and he came out here on his own and must have decided to take a swim. And, Sharon, you were upstairs and you heard the splash and you rushed downstairs and called for help – only Kenny wasn't in –

DOUGLAS What about the couple? You know, the Spanish couple? Do they live in?

TRUDY Yes, but they'll be watching television, they'd never have heard ... And then you came out here, Sharon, you see ...?

SHARON Yes ...

TRUDY And you found Mr Parks floating unconscious in the water –

DOUGLAS In all his clothes?

TRUDY Yes. Good point. We'd better take some of those off him ...

SHARON (*starting at once*) Right ...

TRUDY No, let me finish. And then you dived in, Sharon –

SHARON Was I wearing my wetsuit?

TRUDY No. Well done. You'd better take that off, too.

SHARON What, now?

TRUDY Yes.

SHARON (*softly*) I've got nothing underneath, Mrs Parks.

TRUDY (*angrily*) Sharon, we are talking about murder. If you are going to worry about being done for indecent exposure ...

SHARON (*starting*) Yes, Mrs Parks ... (*She begins to unfasten her belt.*)

TRUDY No, let me finish first. And then, finally, Douglas and I came back from our walk in time to find you trying to revive Vic. But to no avail. How does that sound?

to live in (of servants) to live at one's place of work **to be done for** (*infml*) to be punished for **indecent exposure** crime of showing oneself naked **to no avail** (*lit*) without effect

SHARON Brilliant.

TRUDY (*to Douglas*) All right?

DOUGLAS (*obviously unhappy*) Yes. I don't see an alternative, really, but –

TRUDY (*taking this as agreement*) Sharon, strip off. Douglas, help me with Vic ... Quick as you can, everyone.

The three work in silence, concentrating on their tasks. Sharon takes off her belt, then her hood and flippers. Douglas and Trudy start to undress Vic with difficulty, removing his jacket, shirt, shoes and socks. As they are doing this, they are unaware of the audience that starts to assemble. Through the back gate, Kenny enters. He has the jeep keys, having just returned from the shops. He carries a couple of loose bottles of wine. Behind him comes Ruy, who carries the bulk of their purchase, namely a full case of wine. They stop and watch the proceedings with horrified fascination. Soon after, Marta comes out from the house with a tray, looking for stray dirty glasses. She stops, likewise, to watch suspiciously. Sharon is about to do the final lap of her striptease and remove her wetsuit. She is on the point of doing this when she becomes aware of their audience. She freezes, openmouthed, staring. Trudy and Douglas take a second or so longer to realize. They are on the point of removing Vic's trousers.

(*to Douglas*) Right. You pull off his trousers, while I hold him ...

DOUGLAS (*struggling*) Yes.

It is a difficult operation.

TRUDY God, he's a weight ... Sharon, can you help us?

They struggle again.

DOUGLAS Hang on.

TRUDY He's so ... He's so ... Sharon don't just stand there – please – come and ...

stray (*infml*) not in its proper place, left outside **lap** route around a race-course **to freeze** to become completely motionless

Trudy finally becomes aware of why Sharon has frozen. Douglas is the last to notice. They stand up, guiltily.

KENNY What the hell is going on?

Silence, Vic, released, flops over, very obviously dead.

What have you done to him? What have you done to Vic?

TRUDY (*feebly*) We were just … We were just … undressing him.

KENNY What's happened? He looks dead. Is he dead?

TRUDY (*softly*) Yes, he's dead.

MARTA (*crossing herself, whispering*) Mr Vic!

RUY (*likewise, crossing the carton of wine*) Mr Vic!

KENNY (*softly*) Jesus … I think I'm going to have to phone the police, aren't I?

DOUGLAS Yes, I think you are …

Sharon whimpers.

TRUDY No!

KENNY How did it happen, Trudy? I need to know.

TRUDY Well …

SHARON Well …

DOUGLAS (*stepping forward unexpectedly*) It's all right, leave it to me. (*to Trudy and Sharon*) I'm sorry. There's no other way. There's only one thing worth telling and that's the truth.

KENNY Quite right. It's my experience, in cases like this, that there's absolutely nothing like the truth. Absolutely – nothing like it at all.

Before Douglas can start to explain, ASHLEY BARNES, *a TV floor manager complete with two-way radio, steps on to the floor, appearing unexpectedly and as from nowhere. The lights close down to a small area round him, momentarily.*

ASHLEY (*with great authority*) Sorry, everyone. We need to stop for just a second. Sorry. Bear with us, we won't be two seconds. (*listening to instructions from his earpiece*) Mmm … yes … mmm … hmm-mmm … yes … OK … I see … yes …

to flop to fall in a loose, uncontrolled way **to cross o.s.** to make the sign of the cross **to whimper** to make weak crying noises **two-way radio** *G.* Funksprechgerät

While Ashley listens, the general lighting returns. The actors playing Vic, Douglas, Trudy, Sharon, Kenny, Ruy and Marta have left the stage to be replaced by their counterpart 'TV' actors, who are to be used to mime out scripted events. This switch should have occurred as swiftly and unobtrusively as possible. Although none of the replacement performers concerned are particularly miscast (it is sufficient that they are different), there have been one or two cosmetic improvements. The new Sharon is slim and really quite attractive in her shapely wetsuit. She has shed the helmet and has her hair tied back. Vic is possibly glamorized a little, too, in an anti-hero sort of way. He's certainly less drunk. Ruy and Marta are a shade more 'Spanish'. All the clothing – apart from Sharon's – is similar but not identical to their original counterparts. The ensuing action is as silent as possible, leaving Jill's voice to serve as a 'voice-over' to it.

(*having received final instructions*) OK. I'm afraid we have to go back just to Sharon jumping in the pool.

The actors immediately start to move.

My apologies, everyone, this is purely for cameras. Many apologies. We'll go when you're ready, everyone ... (*to the audience*) Do bear with us once again, ladies and gentlemen. I'm afraid these things do happen. I crave your patience.

The replacement Vic goes off into the house, gathering up his wet clothes as he goes. Replacement Marta precedes him. Replacement Sharon goes off along the pool taking her discarded gear with her. The other replacements go off, Trudy and Douglas following Ruy and Kenny out through the gate. As this

counterpart equivalent **to mime out** to act without speaking **scripted** written down **unobtrusively** (*adv*) not too obvious **miscast** playing the wrong role **shapely** (*adj*) well-shaped, attractive **ensuing** following **to bear with s.b.** to show patience with s.b. **to crave s.th.** (*fml*) to ask for s.th. very urgently **to precede s.b.** to go in front of s.b. **discarded** not needed **gear** *here:* equipment

happens, the real Jill comes on from the house. She is in her smart presenter's outfit. She stands on the patio, waiting. She carries a clipboard. She is in her most tense, unsmiling, professional mood at present.

Sorry, Jill. We'll need to go from the top of that final sequence again.

JILL The final sequence?

ASHLEY From where she jumps in.

JILL OK.

She consults her clipboard. The lighting changes slightly. Although the general area stays lit, there is a bright 'special' on Jill.

ASHLEY (*listening to a final instruction from his earpiece*) OK? Thank you, Jill. (*yelling*) Quiet studio, please. (*to Jill*) In your own time, Jill, whenever you're ready.

He moves back as he speaks. As Ashley goes off, Jill hesitates a second, then moves up a couple of gears in order to do her piece to camera.

JILL And so to the final events of that tragic night. The crew and I had finished for the day and had gone back to our hotel to have dinner. For a description of what followed we must rely, therefore, on the testimonies of first Sharon, the nanny, then Douglas and Trudy, and finally Vic's manager, Kenneth Collins. Piecing together these various eyewitness accounts, the following is almost certainly a true picture of what occured.

As Jill speaks, the previous scene is enacted again. If the facts are different, then so are the performers.

Trudy, in the company of Douglas Beechey, had decided to take a stroll to the beach. Kenneth Collins had walked with Ruy, the gardener, to the local store to buy extra provisions. And whilst Marta, the maid, was preparing supper in the kitchen, Vic sat in the living room relaxing and listening to some of his favourite country and western music.

clipboard small board, with a clip at the top for writing-paper **earpiece** *here:* earphone **to move up a couple of gears** to accelerate, go to a higher level **testimony** formal statement made by a witness **to enact** (*fml*) to play a scene on stage **provisions** food and drink

She pauses for a second to allow the strains of prerecorded background country and western music to filter from the direction of the house. This is not the same as previously heard, probably more romantic. It plays gently under the rest of Jill's speech, accompanying the action that follows. The replacement Sharon enters during the next and stands gazing into the pool and slowly fastening on her diving belt.

Unknown to any of them, it was at this stage that the children's nanny, Sharon Giffin, decided that her life was no longer worth living. She resolved to kill herself. Perhaps the eventual realization that her secret, undeclared passion for Vic Parks could never be reciprocated, combined with a totally naïve misinterpretation of the kindness he had shown to her whilst she worked there, proved too much for this simple, semi-literate girl from Macclesfield. It was her good fortune, even as she fastened on her weighted scuba diver's belt and prepared to jump, that Vic happened to catch sight of her through the open windows. Realizing at once her intention, he rushed out to try and stop her –

The replacement Vic runs out of the house and stops for a minute staring at Sharon.

But he was too late to stop her jumping –

Vic yells silently at Sharon, who jumps into the pool. Vic starts to run to the pool, shedding his shirt and trousers as he does so. He leaps into the pool after her.

What happened next is unclear. Trudy and Douglas arrived back from their walk in time to see two figures struggling in the water in the darkness.

Replacement Douglas and replacement Trudy have entered and hurried at once to the swimming pool, where they haul Sharon from the water, during the next, and bring her round.

strains (of music) *here: G.* Klänge **prerecorded** recorded in advance **to filter** (of sound) to come in faintly **to resolve** to decide **to reciprocate** (*fml*) to return, to give s.th. in return for **semi-literate** (*fml*) hardly able to read and write **weighted** made heavier **to bring s.b. round** to bring s.b. back to consciousness

Sharon, herself, has only the dimmest memory of being hauled from the water in a semi-conscious state. At first, both rescuers concentrated on reviving her, assuming that Vic himself – a strong swimmer and in good physical condition – had no need of assistance. By the time they realized all was not well, it was already too late. In his violent struggle with the desperate, frenzied girl, Vic Parks had received a glancing blow, sufficient to knock him unconscious and allow his lungs to fill with water.

Replacements Trudy and Douglas, under the last, re-enact the sudden realization that Vic is still in the water. They locate his body and start to pull him from the pool. As they do so, replacements Kenny and Ruy appear in the gateway. Ruy carries a box of groceries. Replacement Marta appears in the house doorway. She is wiping her hands on a kitchen towel and has evidently been preparing food.

Despite frantic and repeated efforts, they were too late to save him. When the others returned to the villa, they found themselves little more than powerless spectators, forced to witness the final act of a needless tragedy. That night marked not only the end of a life but the end of a living legend.

During this, Sharon sits exhausted, Trudy and Douglas make efforts to save Vic. Marta, Kenny and Ruy stand watching anxiously. Finally, Douglas looks up from Vic's body and shakes his head. Marta, Kenny and Ruy move in slowly and incredulously. They kneel with the others around the body, forming a moving and well-grouped tableau which then freezes while Jill concludes her speech.

How best to sum up Vic Parks? A man whose life, ironically, ended as violently as it had started. But in between how to describe him? Hero or villain? Latter-day saint or merely late-twentieth-century showman? The arguments will continue.

dim not bright *here:* vague **glancing** (blow) nearly missing, just hitting the side **under** (*TV*) referring to the picture(s) to be seen during the "voice-over" comments **to locate s.th.** to find the position of s.th. **frantic** very excited, frenzied **needless** unnecessary **tableau** carefully arranged group on a stage, standing or sitting without movement **latter-day** (*old use*) modern **argument** quarrel, lively discussion

Perhaps his best epitaph is a piece of advice given spontaneously to a young viewer to whom he said: 'Don't complain to me that people kick you when you're down. It's your own fault for lying there, isn't it?'

She sits in the chair in which she started the play. The music fades out or finishes gently. The lights, from now on, close down on Jill. The others remain frozen and are all but lost in the gloom. By the end of the next, Ashley has reappeared at the edge of the set. Jill's manner now lightens from the solemn/reverent to the fireside/jokey level for her final wind up.

Sad to say, that's the last of *Their Paths Crossed.* If you enjoyed this short series but think that four wasn't *quite* enough, tell you what – why not drop them a line up there and let them know? Them. You know the ones I mean. As for me, I'm off to pastures new but I hope we'll meet again soon. Next week at this time – and quite coincidentally – the start of *The Very Best of Vic* – a series of twelve special programmes featuring selected highlights from his recent series. And don't forget, too, you Vic Parks devotees who happen to be in the London area next month, I'll be co-presenting what's planned to be the first of the Annual Midland Bank Vic Parks Awards for Youth – founded, of course, in memory of the man himself. That's at the Royal Albert Hall on Saturday the 18th. There's still a few seats left. So do try to get along if you can. Remember, it's all in a very good cause. Oh, and incidentally, there's a fabulous country and western line up, too. But in the meantime, that's all from me, Jill Rillington. Bye for now. And mind how you go, won't you? Bye.

Jill smiles into the camera and holds her expression for a second or so. Ashley steps forward into the middle.

ASHLEY Thank you, everyone. Just hold it a minute, please. We're waiting for clearance.

epitaph short comment on a dead person, written on a gravestone **reverent** (*fml*) very respectful **fireside** (*adj*) informal tone one uses at home, sitting by the fireside **wind-up** to sum up and end a statement or meeting **pastures new** (*lit, fml*) new fields of activity **coincidentally** (*adv*) happening by chance **devotee** fan, admirer **to co-present** to be one of the presenters of a show **incidentally** by the way **fabulous** (*infml*) excellent **line up** all the artists to appear in a show, *here: G.* Besetzung **clearance** official OK

He waits. Patiently listening to his earpiece.

JILL (*sweetly, to the audience*) They just have to check that last bit through. See if we've managed to get it right this time. Won't be a second.

A pause. We wait. The actor playing replacement Vic is now sitting up and whistling quietly to himself. The others wait patiently.

ACTOR (*the actor playing replacement Ruy*) Jill ... Jill!

JILL Hallo?

ACTOR I don't know if you noticed, but the second time I came on a tidge later at the end there. I hope that was OK.

JILL (*rather impatiently, the man is obviously a pain*) I'm sure that was fine, David ...

ACTOR I mean, I could do it again if they want it ...

JILL It was fine. I don't think they were on you, then, anyway.

ACTOR (*faintly disappointed*) Oh, right. Fair enough.

Ashley is getting instructions through his earpiece.

ASHLEY (*speaking to the gallery*) Yep ... yeah ... yep ... Great, grand, thank you. Thank you, Jill, thank you very much, everyone. They're very happy with that. Thank you.

The actors leave by the various exits.

JILL (*as she goes, cheerily to the audience*) Bye.

ASHLEY (*briskly and brightly, it is a well-oiled routine*) Right. Ladies and gentlemen, just before you leave – I know you're all dying to get home. One last little request – I know, I've been making requests all evening, but this, I promise you, is my last request for just one vast burst of your really *warmest* applause. That I know only you can give me. We have yet, you see, to record one little further item. Which is, of course, our final credits sequence. That's when all those names of people you've never even *heard* of, doing jobs you don't even know what they *are*, this is when their names go *racing* across your screen while

a tidge a little bit, a shade **to be a pain** (*infml, of a person*) disliked, unwelcome **gallery** the control-room of a studio **cheerily** (*adv*) cheerfully **to be dying to do** (*infml*) to wish strongly to do **burst (of applause)** outbreak (of applause) **credits** the list of actors and other staff at the end of a film

you're busy putting the cat out and couldn't care less anyway. Well, fair enough, but they've got to be there and, more important, one of the names is mine, so when you see that go through – my name is Ashley Barnes, by the way – watch out for it – Ashley Barnes – special loud applause for that, then I get more money, right ... Seriously, as much *warm* applause as you can give us. Let's tell the people at home what a really good time you've had and then who knows, perhaps they'll believe they've had a good one, too. And we'll get a second series after all. All right? So on my signal – we'll be going with the final music ... In just a few seconds. (*Slight pause.*) I hope. (*Pause.*) Yes, here we go. (*He stands. He smiles at the audience. He gets the countdown from the gallery. He holds up his hand and counts down with his fingers, mouthing silently with this*) Five ... four ... three ... two ...

He starts the applause. The final credit music plays under this. The curtain call is taken. The actors leave the stage. The music stops.

Thank you all very much indeed. Goodnight. Get home safely now. (*as he moves away from the floor*) Thank you very much, studio.

The stage lights snap off to be replaced with the house lights.

to take the curtain call (*theatre*) to go out on the stage and bow to the audience
house lights (*theatre*) the lights in the auditorium before and after the show

ADDITIONAL MATERIAL

Alan Ayckbourn: Playwright and Man of the Theatre

Alan Ayckbourn was born in London, on April 12th, 1939, and grew up in the south of England. His father was a musician, his stepfather a bank-manager, his mother wrote fiction for women's magazines. He attended a "Public School", Haileybury College near Hertford, where his interest in acting was awakened. In 1957, he joined Stephen Joseph's "Library Theatre" in Scarborough, a popular seaside-resort on the North Sea coast of Yorkshire. Soon Ayckbourn's talents as a writer and director of plays were discovered, and he gave up acting altogether in 1964. For a few years he worked for the BBC in Leeds as a producer of radio drama but returned to Scarborough in 1970 when his mentor Stephen Joseph had died, to become Artistic Director of the company. With the exception of a two-year period in London (1986-7) as Director of his own company at the National Theatre, and excursions to the London West End or the United States to direct his own plays (or to Oxford University as a Visiting Professor of Contemporary Theatre in 1992), he has spent all his working life in Scarborough. Ayckbourn has received numerous awards, for "Best Comedy of the Year", "Best Play of the Year", "Best Director of the Year" (for his production of *A View from the Bridge*, by American playwright Arthur Miller), and at the beginning of 1997 he was knighted, so that he is now Sir Alan Ayckbourn.

Because he is such a famous and successful playwright people tend to forget that the greater part of his working-time is, in fact, dedicated to activities other than writing: directing plays, his own as well as those of other dramatists, and just "running" his theatre, which involves administration, planning the new season, discovering new plays to be presented at the Stephen Joseph Theatre, finding sponsorship money for productions, hiring actors and other staff, discussing the film programmes which are part of the new Stephen Joseph Theatre's regular activities, and a lot of public relations.

During his tenure as Artistic Director, Ayckbourn has twice had to "move house", from the music room at the Town Library to a school-building in 1976 (where the company was renamed "Stephen Joseph Theatre in the Round"), and in 1996 (because Scarborough Borough Council wanted the school back), a few yards up the road to the present site just across from the station, to a converted cinema, the new "Stephen Joseph Theatre". Nearly all of his over fifty plays were first produced on the "arena stage" of one of these three venues, where the acting area is placed in the middle, with the audience seated all around it, fairly close to the actors.

Ayckbourn is a contemporary dramatist, and he grew up as a writer and man of the theatre with the great names of modern drama, such as the Italian Luigi Pirandello (1867-1936), the Irishman Samuel Beckett (1906-89), or his English compatriot Harold Pinter (*1930). In his early plays (which are no longer available for production) he was very fond of the modernist techniques of theatricality and anti-realism, like some of the absurdist farces characteristic of the "new" English Drama of the late Fifties and the Sixties. But he soon realized that before breaking with traditional concepts one should find out what they are – and prove that one could work with them. So he turned to the realist tradition of drama, which has always been a strong current in the history of English theatre, represented by the later problem plays as well as the comedy of manners, i.e. the (often satirical) comedy of social life that began with Ben Jonson (1572-1637) around 1600, was taken up by dramatists like Wycherley (1640-1716) and Congreve (1670-1729) in the second half of the seventeenth century, by Sheridan (1751-1816) towards the end of the eighteenth century, continued by Oscar Wilde (1854-1900) at the end of the nineteenth century and carried into the twentieth century by such writers as Somerset Maugham (1874-1965) and Noël Coward (1899-1973). What all of these have in common, and share with the French concept of the "well-made play", is their preference for a coherent story and identifiable, reasonably plausible characters.

This does not make Ayckbourn an "old-fashioned" dramatist. His characters are clearly of our time, and the stories he tells us make use of the modern ways of perception which have become familiar to us through our experience of film and television; timewarps, flash-backs and forward projections, multiple alternative actions, dreams and fantasy elements have become regular devices in his plays since the late Seventies. But even when he offers us two rivalling versions of "reality", as in *Man of the Moment*, there is never any doubt as to which of these "realities" is, as it were, "more real" than the other – or to put it the other way round: which of these versions of "reality" is false. His concern is not the definition of reality as such, the discussion of the concept of reality or some such philosophical question. Neither is he trying to explore the concept of "identity", or to work out the results of a basic distrust in such a concept, as – for instance – Harold Pinter does in many of his plays. Alan Ayckbourn's plays are not theatrical enquiries into the nature of "reality" or "identity" or "time" or "being" – they are just case-studies of human behaviour, they are dramatic demonstrations of what people do to other people, and how they often hurt, or fail to understand and appreciate, their fellow human beings. For the benefit of the audience, the individuals shown on the stage must naturally be supposed to be more or less responsible for what they do – otherwise, why should we worry, think, feel about them and their victims? So each character's identity must be pretty well established, i.e. each character must be recognizable as one and the same from the beginning to the end of the story, and the story itself must be coherent and logical so that we can see the connection between the characters' actions and the consequences of these actions and respond to them. In other words, it is Ayckbourn's moral interest which makes the "realist" tradition so important for him.

The point about Ayckbourn's moral concern is, of course, that it does not tempt him to preach or debate and argue, as, for instance, Shaw loved to do. Ayckbourn's moral interest is implicit, hidden in the action – and often not revealed until we have had time to digest, and think about, the performance in the theatre. Our first and spontaneous reaction is laughter, our second reaction (the author hopes) is embarrassment and shame at our laughter, is our realization of the sadness often underlying the comedy.

By the time he took over the Scarborough company in 1970, Ayckbourn had enjoyed his first world-wide success as a playwright: *Relatively Speaking* (1965) is still the best-known and most frequently performed play of his, at least in Germany. Ayckbourn confirmed his fame as a dramatist with more comedies of private life and love, funny plays about families and friends and married couples, in the late Sixties and early Seventies. But in spite of the humour, love and marriage in those early plays turned out to be no guarantee of permanent joy; more and more, gloom crept into Ayckbourn's plays of the Seventies, such as *Absurd Person Singular, Absent Friends,* or *Just Between Ourselves,* although there were still some in which the seriousness was kept at bay, e.g. *The Norman Conquests, Bedroom Farce* or *Taking Steps.* The theme of the injustice of life began to make itself felt in the late Seventies; the sadness and helplessness of the losers as well as the natural ease of the winners, and the surprising reversals of the winner-loser constellation were treated with ironic sympathy in *Joking Apart, Way Upstream, Man of the Moment, The Revengers' Comedies, Wildest Dreams.* The more "political" bent of the Ayckbourn plays of the Eighties, his concern with questions of public morality, has been referred to above, in the *Introduction* to *Man of the Moment.* His latest drama so far, *Things We Do For Love,* at first sight seems a return to the early days of *Relatively Speaking,* a comedy about love won and love lost – although the lovers here are a few years older than in Ayckbourn's first success. At the end of this recent play, however, there are not only the two losers in the war of love who are obviously deeply hurt. The winners as well have not escaped without scars and injuries, and their happiness is overshadowed by feelings of guilt, by their awareness of having inflicted – as a consequence of their actions – pain and suffering on others. It is this theme of pain and suffering, caused intentionally or unwittingly, which connects *Things We Do For Love* with such earlier plays as *Absurd Person Singular, Absent Friends, Just Between Ourselves, Joking Apart, Season's Greetings, Woman in Mind , Henceforward, Wildest Dreams,* and – *Man of the Moment.*

Selected List of Ayckbourn's Plays

Relatively Speaking	Scarborough, July 1965
Absurd Person Singular	Scarborough, June 1972
The Norman Conquests	Scarborough, June 1973
Absent Friends	Scarborough, June 1974
Bedroom Farce	Scarborough, June 1975
Just Between Ourselves	Scarborough, January 1976
Joking Apart	Scarborough, January 1978
Taking Steps	Scarborough, September 1979
Season's Greetings	Scarborough, September 1980
Way Upstream	Scarborough, October 1981
A Chorus of Disapproval	Scarborough, May 1984
Woman in Mind	Scarborough, May 1985
A Small Family Business	London, National Th., May 1987
Henceforward	Scarborough, July 1987
Man of the Moment	Scarborough, August 1988
The Revengers' Comedies	Scarborough, June 1989
Wildest Dreams	Scarborough, May 1991
Time of My Life	Scarborough, April 1992
Communicating Doors	Scarborough, February 1994
Things We Do For Love	Scarborough, April 1997
Comic Potential	Scarborough, June 1998
House & Garden	Scarborough, June 1999

Suggestions for Further Reading

For information on current productions check the Stephen Joseph Theatre website: www.sjt.uk.com

Ian Watson (ed.), *Conversations with Ayckbourn* (London: Faber, ^{2}1988)
Michael Billington, *Alan Ayckbourn* (London et al: Macmillan, ^{2}1990)
Malcolm Page, *File on Ayckbourn* (London: Methuen, 1989)

A Video Documentation on Ayckbourn and the Stephen Joseph Theatre was made at Hamburg University English Department, using material shot in Scarborough; copies are available from
Institut für Anglistik und Amerikanistik
Von-Melle-Park 6, 20146 Hamburg (c.o. Professor Dr. E. Tiedje).

Interview with Alan Ayckbourn on *Man of the Moment*

(E.T.: Egon Tiedje; A.A.: Alan Ayckbourn)

E.T.: *Man of the Moment* has a singular in the title although there are **two** men really ...

A.A.: Yes, yes, they are very different men. Douglas has "Man of the Moment" thrust upon him as the result of an act of heroism which was more spontaneous than planned, and was forgotten over night by the press as they moved on to something else. It's a play about the press, it's a play about the media really. It's about how the media are driven by the public's need for sensation, about the fact that it's always more interesting to learn bad news than good news. (There are all the jokes about people trying to start "good" newspapers – in the sense that the news is all good – and how they fail immediately, because in the end no one really wants to read them.) The play is intended as a contrast between two people. It's based (very very loosely) upon the famous Great Train Robbery, in 1963, when the mail train from London to Edinburgh was robbed. The men who did the deed were a miscellaneous group: antique dealers, small-time crooks and so on. They got away with ten million, the biggest haul possible at the time, the biggest ever. When they'd stopped the train one of them had coshed the driver, who later and quite quietly died of that injury. But it was the robbers who were made heroes, and not the driver, who was completely unknown. And I realised that throughout our history – whether it be Billy the Kid, Ned Kelly, Dick Turpin – most of our folk heroes are actually people who killed for a living; they were often quite dangerous, antisocial people. We have a love of that sort of thing: Everyone's heard of Jack the Ripper, but nobody remembers (apart from a very few people) who his victims were.

to thrust upon to force s.o. to have s.th. **mail train** special train carrying only letters, parcels, etc. **miscellaneous** mixed **antique dealer** person buying and selling old furniture, paintings, etc. **small-time crook** (*infml*) not a serious criminal **haul** (*infml*) stolen goods **to cosh s.b.** (*infml*) to knock out s.b. **Billy the Kid** American outlaw, the hero of many films, shot dead by Sheriff Pat Garrett, his former friend, at Fort Sumner, New Mexico, in 1881 **Ned Kelly** Edward Kelly, Australian outlaw of the late 1870's, hanged at Melbourne in 1880 **Dick Turpin** English highwayman (a person who robs travellers of their belongings), hanged at York in 1739 **Jack the Ripper** the name an unidentified mass murderer gave himself, who in 1888-9 brutally killed prostitutes in the East End of London but was never caught

In fact he was faceless and no one's ever found out who he was; but the women, whom we do know about, are of no real interest to us – which is a sad reflection on our society. So I decided to write a play about it. About two men: one a bank clerk, who is very uninteresting but who had years before tried to stop a bank robbery, and the other, the bank robber concerned, who having paid his so-called "debt to society", is released from prison through good behaviour and goes on to become a mega-star, a huge television personality, doing children's shows and chat-show programmes: he's an immensely desirable entity simply because (that old cliché!) he is in some way or other "loved by the camera". As for Douglas, the bank clerk, who was indeed instrumental in the robber's capture and who had subsequently married the girl who was injured in the bank robbery (she had lost an ear in the shooting), both he and the girl are totally forgotten.

And the play's about what happens when a television company brings them together hoping (I think) that sparks will fly when Douglas, the victim, is confronted by the man who injured his wife and has caused so much pain and fear since. The interesting thing about crime, and something that's very rarely mentioned in the media, in the press or on film or on television or even in plays, is the trauma that follows the crime: people seem to get over it very quickly, but in fact they don't, and some never. The play was about this, as well. Of course, the truth of the matter is that Douglas does *not* confront Vic, he's his greatest fan. Douglas is a Christian, Douglas has "turned the other cheek", and Vic, the villain, for most of the play looks like getting away with it ... much to the frustration of the television presenter who's trying to produce a confrontational programme. Anyone who's been on television (as I have quite a lot of times) knows about that. On two or three occasions people have whispered to me in commercial breaks, "Can you make it a bit more argumentative, can you disagree more, it's a bit boring, this programme"... Television is really only for people who disagree, as far as I can make out. People watching it slump asleep

reflection (on) criticism (of) **to release** to allow a prisoner to go free **chat-show** on German TV called "Talkshow" **desirable** much liked, much wanted **entity** (*n.*) being, G. Wesen **instrumental (in):** (*fml*) helpful, useful **subsequently** (*adv*) afterwards **spark** very small piece of burning material flying from a fire **to turn the other cheek** (*bible*) to offer the other cheek **confrontational** having the quality of, or leading to, a confrontation **commercial break** pause for advertising in a TV programme **argumentative** ready to disagree **to slump** to drop down

if they ever have three people on all of whom have the same view. People say, "Why do you always have television programmes where politicians come on and argue?" And the TV presenters say, "Because politicians know that in the end that's the only entertainment factor people want". So *Man of the Moment* is a play about that, and how in the end the people trapped in the middle have made the wrong choices about which man they follow ... I hope it has a message, I hope it has a moral point. But it's also a comedy, and it's again one of my plays in which you need very carefully to walk the tightrope between the comedy and the tragedy ... they exist together. These plays- ... when I'm directing them they need directing with extreme seriousness, for the comedy to surface of its own accord as soon as it meets an audience.

E.T.: Jill, I think, makes a basic mistake that many media people make: They confuse the ability to have feelings with the ability to *express* them adequately, and that's one of the problems she has with Douglas.

A.A.: Oh yes, she's a monster, Jill really is ... I know "where she's coming from", as they say, in that she's a media woman in (in this case) the BBC, a huge media structure which is still largely male-oriented, and women in those establishments have to fight very very hard to achieve what men achieve far more easily. It's not to say they don't do it, but quite often it creates a certain toughening of the persona, and often only the most aggressive of the women succeed. Jill is based on one that I met; she is almost paranoid, actually. She feels that the whole institution is there to bring her down. She's really, in one sense, the worst type of interviewer as she's imposing her personality on the programme and fails to listen to what people are trying to say. She doesn't listen to Douglas; she's so much part of the Vic Parks world that she's already decided what Douglas is. And I suppose there's something else. The play says: Never never make prejudgments about people, they will always surprise you, by a degree of sensitivity, of understanding

to argue to quarrel, to insist on one's point **tightrope** rope fastened above ground, on which an acrobat walks or dances **to walk the tightrope** (*fig*) *G.* einen Balanceakt vollführen **adequately** (*adv*) good enough, sufficiently **male-oriented** dominated by men **establishment** *here:* institution **to toughen (s.b.)** to become (or make) stronger **persona** (*psychology*) the impression or image of oneself one shows to others **paranoid** unhealthily suspicious **to impose s.th. on s.b.** to compel s.b. to accept s.th. **prejudgement** harsh opinion formed in advance **sensitivity** awareness and understanding of other people's feelings

that you didn't think them capable of. One has to be very careful about the contemptuous dismissal of people whom you think you've put into a pigeonhole. Very dangerous. And as for people like Douglas, ... I hope by the end of the play (if the play is working right) we, the audience, who laughed when he arrived, really want him to take us with him when he goes, because we no longer want to stay in this place with a man like Vic, who is as violent and dangerous, who has done so much damage to people. He's violent emotionally as I use him in the play... I could have made him do acts of physical violence to people, but I didn't want that, because that sends out all sorts of messages. The violence he uses is towards the baby-sitter, Sharon, who loves him. He uses that love as a terrible weapon against her, and it's the most awful scene he has with her, but I think it says much more than – you know – a single punch on the nose would ever say.

E.T.: You have been called a moralist occasionally; I mean, that's a rather big word, perhaps you would say that at least you aren't a moralist all of the time ...

A.A.: I'm an entertainer, I'm (I hope) a storyteller. I hope that my plays are always moral, but some of them are more overtly moral ... I hate to make claims about any of my work really, I leave it to other people. But I think some of them do verge on being morality tales, certainly plays like *Man of the Moment*, certainly *A Small Family Business* (which was written very near that time), even *A Chorus of Disapproval* (which was again all part of that same era) ... they're all quite large-scale for me, plays about people's actions and the choice of actions, and how their actions often come back to haunt them later in the play.

E.T.: I was not thinking of "moralist" in the theological sense of sin and virtue and good and evil as abstract qualities but rather in the narrower, pragmatic sense of "what we do to people and what people do to us", in that sense.

contemptuous very unkind and disrespectful, *G.* verächtlich **dismissal** refusal to consider (any longer), *G.* Abweisung **to put into a pigeonhole** *here:* (*metaph.*) to put into a category **overtly** (*adv*) openly **to make claims (about)** to make statements (about s.th.) which one expects to be accepted as true **to verge on** to be close to **morality tale** from "morality play", a religious play, esp. of the 15th and 16th centuries, which shows personifications of sin and virtue and good and evil spirits fighting for the soul of man **large-scale** large *here:* referring to characters larger than life, i.e. not as ordinary as in other plays **to haunt** to visit (and follow s.b. like a ghost) **virtue** moral goodness *G.* Tugend **pragmatic** concerned with the practical side of things

A.A.: That's true. "By your own actions, you know, shall you be judged" ... It's very easy to make everything very tidy and say, Ah well, that man did the wrong action in Act One, and we must make sure he gets it in Act Three. But the interesting footnote to the story behind the play is that the man who coshed the driver of the train, Buster Edwards, indeed became – in a much smaller way – a celebrity. There was a film made about him, starring Phil Collins; he became a flower-seller at Waterloo Station, and people used to come and have a look at him: See, that's the train robber. He was a minor celebrity. But he hanged himself only a year or so ago ... it's a very strange and sad end to the story. Heaven knows if it was in any way connected, I don't know. The moralist in me would try and link it. But I really know none of the robbers, I've used the events only to inspire a story which in the end has no reference to the actual robbery at all.

E.T.: The interesting thing about the television people in the play is that they don't even notice the truth when they see it.

A.A.: Well, they don't ... they tend to take a line, and it's often a line that suits them; I remember when I was first interviewed (when *Relatively Speaking* had become such a big success) and the critic said, "Could I say that you've risen from abject poverty to ...?" and I said, "Well no, I'm working for the BBC actually, and I don't think they'd like it if I said I was working in abject poverty". They said, "What a pity, it'll make a better story". They're always looking for angles to make a better story. You understand it. But ... it ain't nothing to do with the truth quite often.

(*Stephen Joseph Theatre*, Scarborough, August 19th, 1996)

"By your own actions"... an allusion to the preaching of Jesus Christ in the New Testament, cf. Matthew 7 **celebrity** celebrated person, famous person **a film... starring Phil Collins** *Buster* (UK, 1988); there was also a very successful German TV production, which managed to suppress the death of the engine-driver (*Die Gentlemen bitten zur Kasse*, NDR, 1966) **reference (to)** *here:* connection (with) **abject** (*fml*) very low and miserable **poverty** lack of wealth, state of being poor **it ain't nothing (to do with)** (*nonstandard*) it is/has nothing (to do with)

Interview with "Douglas Beechey" *

J.S.: Douglas is a type which I think English people – wherever they are – recognize. He's that sort of slightly downtrodden, rather modest man who just works nine to five, fifty-odd years, and then retires. A man of no great ambition, but a man who'd never dream of taking anything from anybody.

E.T.: I understand from the book by Michael Billington, the former *Guardian* drama critic, that during the run of the original production in 1988 people actually talked to you in Scarborough, in the street, and congratulated you on your honesty, and standing up for decency, etc.

J.S.: Yes, it's extraordinary really that people sometimes aren't able to separate the performer and the character, and Douglas was obviously such a ... warm isn't quite the right word, but ... he looked approachable as a character. He looked like an ordinary sort of man that you could go up and talk to, and people in the street did come up and talk to me as if I was Douglas ... which was rather alarming actually because I am not at all like Douglas.

E.T.: But it was a compliment on your acting ...

J.S.: Oh, it was a good sign from the point of view of having given a plausible performance. But I think with Douglas it was the character as well as the acting: you don't very often on stage see the embodiment of goodness in such a pure form as Douglas showed it, and I think people responded to that by thinking that was something they wanted to identify with, and they wanted to come up and say, "Yes, we think you you're right", or "You did well", or whatever.

* The actor Jon Strickland played Douglas in the original production of *Man of the Moment*.

downtrodden (*lit*) treated without respect by those in power **to retire** to stop working and get a pension ***The Guardian*** one of the great national newspapers, of moderately left views **run** the period of time during which performances of a play are shown at a theatre **to stand up for** to support (in public) **decency** the quality of being socially and morally acceptable **approachable** easy to talk to **embodiment (of)** representative, essence (of) **to respond (to)** to react favourably (to)

E.T.: What did you find the biggest challenge in acting a character as "good" as Douglas?

J.S.: I think it's always very hard to play a slightly boring, good man, you know; people always like watching the villain of the piece, and actors like playing the villains, because it's very hard not to make a man whose life is apparently boring just as boring to watch. You have two (or two and a half) hours to do the play, and that's too long to just play a boring man, I think the audience would probably go home. So I had to find some way of making him guileless, not just "good", but making him somebody who had no concept of being other than he was. I think the audience will act like Vic who constantly looks for some hidden side of Douglas ... he can't believe that Douglas is as he is. Vic asks Douglas a couple of times what he actually wants. But Douglas doesn't want anything. He really doesn't want anything. And I think the journey the audience make with Douglas, which you have to try and get them to make, is for it to slowly dawn on them as well that there isn't a hidden plan, a hidden agenda. So you keep them hooked in for a while with them thinking, like Vic, that Douglas is going to reveal a plot to blackmail, or to do something strange. But then gradually it dawns on the audience that this man is just what he says he is: a man with no thoughts of revenge and no desire to "do" Vic ... he just wants to meet him. The only slight thing that Douglas does want is to lay this ghost to rest because it's still haunting his wife.

E.T.: But he's not an unhappy person.

J.S.: No, he's not unhappy ... I think that's what people find very hard, because we're just not used to seeing people quite as straightforward as Douglas on stage. And that is a challenge to play, I suppose, because as an actor you also want to try and flesh out characters and suggest the dark and hidden corners of them, but with Douglas I couldn't do that, because the minute you started making him too interesting then he stopped working as a character ... I mean he's not a two-dimensional character, he's fully written, but he's not a man with vast secret acres to explore.

(*Scarborough, August 20th, 1996*)

challenge problem to solve **guileless** honest, sincere, with no intention to deceive **to dawn on s.b.** to become clear to s.b.'s mind **agenda** list of topics (at a meeting), list of things one wants to do **hooked in** *here:* having one's attention caught, being interested **to reveal** to lay open, show **plot** secret plan **blackmail** (act of) getting money from s.b. by threats **to do s.b.** (*infml*) to cheat s.b. **to flesh s.th. out** to add substance to s.th.